A Wild Coast
and
Lonely

by Rosalind Sharpe Wall

Big Sur Pioneers

WIDE WORLD PUBLISHING/TETRA

front cover: *photo of Big Sur coastline*
                  by Rosalind Sharpe Wall

title page: *View of coast looking south from Palo Colorado.*
                  Rocky Creek and Bixby Landing beyond. 1900.
                  —Collection of Frank Trotter.

The title of this book, *A Wild Coast & Lonely,* is taken from the *Ballad of the South Coast* by Lillian Bos Ross. Permission to reprint it here was given by Harrydick Ross.

Wide World Publishing/Tetra
P.O. Box 476
San Carlos, CA 94070

3rd printing 2000
Printed in the United States of America.

ISBN: 0-933174-60-8

Library of Congress Cataloging–in–Publication Data

Wall, Rosalind Sharpe
    A Wild Coast and Lonely—Big Sur Pioneers /
    Rosalind Sharpe Wall
    p.   cm.
    Bibliography: p.
    ISBN 0-933174-83-7 : $9.95
    1. Frontier and pioneer life — California —Big Sur Region. 2. Big
Sur Region (Calif.) — History.
    I. Wall, Rosalind Sharpe.
    A Wild Coast and Lonely—Big Sur Pioneers. II. Title.
    F869, B63W34 1989   88-36671
    979.4'76—dc19   CIP

To my mother, Frida G. Sharpe,
for whom this book was written.

This book has been a long time in the making.

I first conceived of writing it when I was only eleven years old, in 1930. This was because I was annoyed by the fact that hundreds of tourists came flocking down the old county road looking for the tragic protagonists of the Jeffers' poems and finding them, they thought, in every old ranch-house, especially ours. Robinson Jeffers' *Thurso's Landing* had just come out and our house, the old Gilkey ranch-house built in 1875, was its locale.

My mother was a passionate admirer of Jeffers and so was I, even at that early age. I was especially drawn to him perhaps because I lived in the very heart of his country, and he seemed to me, even then, to lend it a voice, to echo its spirit. I remember my mother reading Jeffers aloud after dinner by the light of the kerosene lamp, sitting in her huge Philippine throne chair and wearing a red lace evening gown, left over from formal regimental dinner parties in Manila. (My father was a retired Army officer.) She read beautifully and had a marvelous voice, but unfortunately we did not have tape recorders in those days.

Frida Sharpe was an omnivorous reader and a former school teacher. She had a branch library at Mill Creek (now Bixby Creek) and I believe she was almost its only patron. She got books by the boxful from Salinas via the mail-stage and devoured them voraciously. During the winter months when the stage could not get through on account of storms and slides she read the Encyclopedia from cover to cover.

She said to me years later, "It was terribly frustrating to be teeming with information in that lonely canyon with no one to talk to." (She and my father had different interests.)

Mother also ran the Sur post-office; the only other post-office on the coast was Arborlado, at the Post ranch, which was at the very end of the wagon-road three miles past Big Sur. She also helped run, with my father, a tourist resort called Rainbow Lodge.

My mother discovered Jeffers long before anyone else had ever heard of him. This was when she stumbled upon *Californians*, a slim volume of romantic, rhymed, somewhat Wordsworthian verse, strongly influenced by old Scotch ballads. They were based partly on tales of people living in the mountains behind Santa Barbara, partly on the isolated cattle ranches and lonely mountain and canyon fastnesses of the Sur. This region, known today as the Big Sur country, had been virtually unheard-of until Jeffers' *Tamar* and *The Roan Stallion* appeared in the late '20s. People seldom went down there except to visit Pfeiffer's resort in the summer. The inhabitants were regarded as primitive rustics who turned up in town once a year in spring-wagons for supplies or else drove their cattle, lowing and bawling, into Monterey over the old coast road.

I remember that on these annual cattle drives, people in the Sur were warned in advance and we all drew our blinds, so as not to distract the cattle.

One time Tom Doud's cattle, including a prize bull, broke loose and ran madly down Alvarado Street, throwing people into a panic and scattering them in every direction. The bull, in fact, jumped into a parked sports car, to add to the confusion.

To those of us who lived on the coast, it was never called Big Sur. It was simply The Coast, as though it were the only coast in the world. It was the Spaniards who had labelled it the Sur, Sur simply being the Spanish word for South. By it they referred to the entire coast lying south of Carmel Mission. Early American settlers identified themselves more precisely in terms of where they lived: Palo Colorado, Garapata, Soberanes

Creek, Little Sur, Big Sur, Big Creek, Limekiln Creek, Lucia, etc.. People living in the northern sector of the coast felt relatively little connection with the Big Sur folk; they were too far away and we seldom saw them. It took all day to get there.

Although the Santa Lucia mountains between Carmel and San Luis Obispo were 130 miles in length, the area under consideration — the one now called Big Sur — started at Carmel River, just below Carmel Mission, and ended near Lucia, 65 miles to the South. This was a mountain country, fissured into by deep redwood canyons. Each canyon was different, had its own history and atmosphere; its own *ambiente*. The Big Sur was merely one of these canyons, although it was the biggest one. However, it assumed importance in 1910 when Florence Swetnam Pfeiffer decided in a pique to charge board and room to the many travellers who stopped there, eating them out of house and home, thus accidentally establishing the famed Pfeiffer's Resort.

After the highway went through in 1937, the entire area south of Carmel became known as the Big Sur. Pfeiffer's Resort, which had been in the Pfeiffer's own home, was replaced by the slick and modern Big Sur Lodge at Pfeiffer Big Sur State Park. Later, to add further reinforcement to the place name, avant-garde writer Henry Miller wrote *Big Sur and the Oranges of Heironymous Bosch*. He had settled there in 1944 as a refugee from occupied France, first staying with Lynda Sargent at the old Coastlands Trails Club which is now Nepenthe, then moving to Partington Ridge. In the 1950s the Beat writer, Jack Kerouac, came out with a book called *Big Sur*. Its locale was actually Bixby Creek (my old home at Mill Creek) and he went down there, ridiculously enough, in a taxi-cab. Jack Kerouac never even visited the Big Sur.

I loved my country and I loved Robinson Jeffers, but I hated the notoriety that had come upon it as a result of Jeffers' tragic narratives. I lived in the center of the Jeffers country and,

from time to time, the Jeffers stopped by our ranch with their
twin sons, Garth and Donnan, who were two years older than I
was. I was, in every sense, surrounded by Jeffers — his
landscape, his atmosphere, his characters (or rather those
whom people mistook for his characters, including ourselves)
and every canyon, every rock, every mountain, every thrust of
the surf, every circling hawk spoke of Jeffers and his immortal
lines such as "O noble Pico Blanco, steep sea wave of marble..."
or "This coast crying out for tragedy, like the spirit of all
beautiful places..."

Pico Blanco was the great Ventana peak overtowering the Little
Sur, a mountain sacred to the Esselen Indians and the center of
their creation myth. Twice a year, at the time of the equinoxes,
they gathered there for ceremonies, worship and traditional
dances.

As a child I never felt alone: I was always being watched; the
land itself or something within it was always aware of me,
always watching me. Often I wished it wouldn't. I had no
secret or private thoughts. I was transparent as glass. But as
the late Frank Post wrote in his diary, "Many a time, in the
deep woods, my Great Protector was with me, always watching
me, standing guard over me."

My mother often spoke of "the inner content of the coast hills."
She felt a Presence there - a nameless and inhuman one,
neither benign nor malign. It was, perhaps, the universe itself
or, as Jeffers put it, "the inhuman magnificence of things."

Thurso's Landing, the poem which was eventually to lead to
this little book, came out in 1930 when the highway was being
built with convict labor. By this time my father had build a
place he called the Stone House (later Bixby Inn) at the
northern end of Rainbow Bridge (Bixby Creek Bridge) which
was not quite completed. Tourists would drive this far down
the new highway, then come flocking down our hill, over the

old precipitous country road, looking for the Jeffers characters. As our house was the locale of the principal scene in _The Loving Shepherdess_ and was also the infamous Thurso ranch-house it drew an undue share of attention. People identified my father with the mean old rancher who refused to give shelter to the dying, pregnant shepherdess, Claire Walker, and my mother with Helen Thurso who had killed her paralyzed husband with bichloride of mercury tablets.

Frida Sharpe was vastly amused by all this and had a lovely time pulling the legs of tourists, often adding dramatic touches of her own or even inventing stories wholesale. But I was a humorless child and failed to appreciate this. I determined that when I grew up I would write a book about the Coast and its inhabitants as it actually was.

But my interests and perspective inevitably shifted when I began to go to school in Carmel in the winter-time, living at the ranch only in the summer during the tourists season. However, it was to be re-activated at Monterey High School when I met John L.D. Roberts II, the grandson of the old coast doctor who was responsible for the building of the Carmel-San Simeon Highway.

John, an aspiring and gifted young poet at 16, was as devoted to Jeffers as I was, and, through his grandfather, had his roots in the Sur coast. He and I spent many week-ends exploring deserted homesteads in the Sur, visiting old-timers, but above all listening to the fascinating tales told by his grandfather. Dr. Roberts and his wife, Edith, often went down to the Little Sur where he had built a primitive little cabin, _Cyclone_, to get away from civilization, modern times, and his huge concrete mansion overlooking Del Monte beach. (Dr. Roberts was the founder of the city of Seaside.) Here, cooking on a wood-stove and listening to the sound of the Little Sur River and his many water wheels just outside the door, he could remember his days as a young country doctor, riding down the coast on horseback medicine bag in hand, tending the sick, or more frequently going down in an old two-wheel cart drawn by his horse, Daisy.

Although Dr. Roberts was proud of the highway he had created, which had been the dream of his life-time, he too hankered for the good old days of his young manhood.

Now the beauty of the big Sur coast belonged to the world. But for us old-timers a saga had ended, a ballad had struck its last note.

I have deliberately ended this book with World War II when the road closed after Pearl Harbor, for although the highway inevitably brought big changes, its spirit did not change essentially until after World War II. The world and life that grew up in its place was quite different from the one that is described in this book and possibly deserves a book of its own.

Although the days and people I remember are gone forever, the beauty remains unmarred and, for the most part, untouched.

May it so remain. May its beauty be, as Robinson Jeffers said, imperishable.

Acknowledgements

The material found in this book was based almost entirely on interviews with oldtimers and sons and daughters of the original homesteaders of the Sur coast in addition to my own personal memories, for I grew up on a ranch at Mill Creek (Bixby Creek) in pre-highway days. Those who gave to me so generously of their time and recollections as well as lending me photographs include: Harvey Abbott, Jess Artellan, Vesta Bauman, Helen Brown, Rogelio "Roche" Castro, Elayne Hopper Chanslor, William Colby, John B.R. Cooper III, Alvin Dani, Kate Pfeiffer Dani, Dr. Jaime de Angulo, Gui de Angulo, Harry Downie, Amelie Elkinton, Esther Pfeiffer Ewoldsen, Gene Fitzpatrick, Josie Simoneau Fussell, Alta Bixby Gregg, Corbett Grimes, Electa Dani Grimes, Florence Hogue, Jimmy Hopper, Robinson and Una Jeffers, Dr. Benjamin Kurtz, Amy Melissa Gilkey Miller, Dr. John Murphy, Eugenia Murray, Monsignor Michael D. O'Connell, Steve and Annie Sousa Patterson, Susan Porter, Charles Francis Post, Joseph W. Post, William Post III, Dr. John L.D. Roberts, John L.D. Roberts II, Lillian Bos Ross, Harrydick Ross, West Smith, Sadie Starrett, Lynda Sargent, Burt Tolerton, David Tolerton, Janet Tolerton, Frank Trotter, Elizabeth Hogue Van der Pleogh, Ruby Gear Woicekowiski, Steve and Alice Post Yaeger.

I am especially indebted to Frank Trotter for lending me his father's — Sam Trotter's — journal; to Esther Pfeiffer Ewoldsen for permitting me to read her mother's — Florence Swetnam Pfeiffer's — account of the Pfeiffer family; and to the late Charles Francis Post for lending me his diary which is, in itself, a work of poetry.

In addition, I am deeply grateful to Alice Kent, Helen Taylor, Flavia Flavin Edgren, Virginia McGrath, Kate V. Schlepp, Mitchell Chanelis, Burt Tolerton, John L.D. Roberts II, Cressandra Hopkins, and Kipp Finn for their active help and encouragement in making this book a reality. Last but not least I wish to mention my professors at Sonoma State: Drs. Martin Blaze, Helen Dunn, Gerald Haslam and Gerald Rosen, who saw this book in its original version and permitted me to use it as a creative project in lieu of a formal M.A. thesis, albeit in much abbreviated form.

—*Rosalind Sharpe Wall*

CONTENTS

View of Coast looking south from Palo Colorado. Rocky Creek and Bixby Landing. Circa 1900. The telephone line led to only one phone—at Point Sur Lighthouse.

— Collection of Frank Trotter

I.

The Indians
are the
Only Real Ghosts

I was not only close to the land but to its history — Indian, Spanish, Mexican, American — and it could be said that the land of my childhood was a land of walking ghosts — or so I interpret it now when everyone is dead and I am one of the few remaining heirs to its recollections.

T he beauty of the Big Sur Coast is legend in America. Thousands of tourists visit it every year on their way between San Francisco and Los Angeles and even a popular camper has been named the Big Sur. There is no town there, no town of Big Sur — only spectacular mountains, sea-cliffs, redwoods, and a few restaurants and tourists resorts. The highway is a lonely one with no billboards, no hot dog stands. There are, in fact, few places to stop for food or gasoline along the entire length of the highway, which is 130 miles between Carmel and San Luis Obispo. It is still a lonely country, sparsely settled, despite the highway.

Noted after the end of World War II as the haven of an avant-garde art colony centering around the controversial figure of Henry Miller, author of the then-banned books *Tropic of Cancer* and *Tropic of Capricorn*, Big Sur drew thousands of curiosity seekers who were disappointed to find that the much-publicized colony, which had made headlines in the *San Francisco Examiner* in a series of sensational articles by Clint Mosher, was all but non-existent. Henry Miller did live there; he had migrated from occupied France in 1944, and after the war ended, was joined by a handful of friends including Gilbert Niemann, the translator of Lorca's *Blood Wedding* from the original Spanish, Walker Winslow, who wrote *If A Man Be Mad* under the pen-name Harold Maine, Franz Sandow, the sculptor, and Emil White, a Jewish refugee from Poland, who was Henry's secretary and also a painter of primitive landscapes which he did in silk-screen. Bezalel Schatz, who had inherited from his father the principal art school in Jerusalem, was there too, and did the silk-screen illustrations for Henry Miller's $100 book *Into the Night Life* (only 100 copies were printed) which was an extract from *The Tropic of Capricorn*. But these quiet, unassuming, hard-working folk were by no means the colorful, sexy, and anarchic bohemians who had been depicted in numerous articles (commencing with Mildren Edy Brady's "The Cult of

Sex and Anarchy" which was published in *Harper's* magazine) and were, indeed, tame in comparison to the beatniks and hippies who succeeded them.

They were *noisier*, however.

As Douglas Madsen of Big Sur said to me once, "Rosalind, do you remember the good old days? We had so much fun, dancing and drinking beer and going to costume parties on Hallowe'en at *Nepenthe*. All these people do is sit around in silence, puffing marijuana."

The Big Sur today does not live up to its legendary reputation. Artists, writers, and latter-day hippies do exist and there are even marijuana growers there, but they are rare and not very flashy. It is mainly the habitat of the very rich plus a dwindling handful of old-timers.

Curiously, even as the fame of Big Sur has spread, its colorful pioneer history has been forgotten. The once isolated, somber and mysterious landscape made famous by the narrative poems of Robinson Jeffers has vanished along with tales of feuds and murders and the sight of seagulls following in the wake of horse-drawn ploughs. (Tony Brazil, near Hurricane Point just south of Bixby Creek, was still ploughing his fields with horses years after the highway opened.) During wagon road days — and it was still a wagon road, a couple of ruts with grass growing between, occasionally smoothed out by graders, despite the fact that motor cars used it — this region was so identified with the Jeffers poems as to seem synonymous with them and people who went down there in search of their passionate protagonists were certain that they had found them. In reality, Jeffers had not drawn his characters (save in one or two instances), nor his thematic material from the Sur Coast, but there were distinct similaries in mode and feeling, occasionally even in details; enough similarity to cause confusion. For example, in "Apology for Bad Dreams" Jeffers described a woman who punished a horse by tying it by its nostrils to a tree; later the horse killed her. Jeffers claimed this was based on fact. But this was quite unusual! He said he had witnessed her punishment of the horse. Today, if and when the history of the region is mentioned it is usually described in terms of the Jeffers poems. Indeed, it has been said, and with truth, that never has a poet been so identified with his locale as Jeffers has with the huge mountains, somber redwood canyons and lonely ranch-houses of the Sur in pre-highway days.

State Highway Number One, also known as the Cabrillo Highway, was originally called the Carmel-San Simeon, then the Roosevelt Highway. Today it is simply part of State Highway Number One. The dream of an old Coast doctor, Dr. John L.D. Roberts who had once walked the entire length of the Santa Lucia mountains on foot and by trail, construction on it began in the 1920s during the Governor Richardson administration. It went as far as Anderson Creek, then further construction was abandoned until 1929-1930. Dr. Roberts, with the help of Senator Rigdon, campaigned for more funds and succeeded also in getting free convict labor through a friend who was a prison warden.

Dr. Roberts was the one to cut the ribbon in the ceremony at Bixby Creek Bridge on July 3, 1937, when it was opened to tourist traffic. The most spectacular stretch of Coast in all of California had been made accessible to the public, but with this an era ended forever. I did not attend the ceremony, as I was opposed to "progress" — a word of which my father was particularly fond. Many Coast ranchers, including himself, expected to make millions from tourists trade along the new highway. John Roberts II did not attend the ceremony either, despite his reverence for his grandfather; but I believe he was away that year.

The land settled in the very late 1850s,1860s, and early 1870s by

pioneer homesteaders had been distinctly a land apart —
insular, primitive, and possessed of a distinct regional
atmosphere. Noted for its violence, it bore a certain family
resemblance to the Ozarks where feuds, as in the Sur, were
common. (Most of the feuds in the Sur were relatively harmless,
but several were fatal, including one between the Bowmans, the
Krenkels, and Hearst's riders at San Simeon.)

Accessible only by trail and wagon road, its lonely inhabitants
raised cattle for their living, also sheep and hogs. Only those
who lived close to town, such as the Hatton ranch, the Allen
ranch and other places at Carmel Highlands, could have dairy
farms or truck gardens. Alexander M. Allen, however, who
raised cattle, also made a tourist business out of what later
became Point Lobos State Park. In the 1880s and 1890s, the
population of the Coast swelled to several thousand due to a
boom in the tanbark and lumber industries, plus limekilns, gold
and silver mines; but after the turn of the century most of this
had shut down except for the limekiln at Mill Creek (Bixby
Creek) owned by the Monterey Lime Company. The high cost of
shipping made these industries unprofitable. Consequently,
most of the canyons were left deserted, littered with abandoned
houses, shacks and barns, and sad fruit orchards struggling
against the sea-wind.

Most of the families left in the Sur were interrelated; everyone
knew everyone and it was like a big clan. Once a year the
population gathered at various ranches for big spring roundups
which, like those at the Cooper ranch, lasted three days at a
time. These were, however, almost the only social occasions
aside from the annual apple-harvesting bee at Post's. The rest
of the year people lived in isolation, seldom seeing their
neighbors and going to town only once a year for supplies. In
early days supplies came down by boat from San Francisco, but
after the wagon road was built in 1881, people went to
Monterey for them. In certain remote areas, such as in the
mountains around Lucia, the stronghold of the Harlans and

the Danis, there were women who had never been to town in their entire lives. Their supplies came by boat and were dumped in the surf at Big Creek. Sometimes boat-load after boat-load turned over in the waves. They had to struggle out to rescue it. When they did go to town they went to King City, via the Jolon Pass, rather than through Big Sur to Monterey. Although the trip to King City took two days, it was closer.

Feuds were frequent in the Coast hills, as were tales of murder, insanity, suicide and adultery. These tales grew to legendary proportions when the Jeffers poems made the region famous. However, the actual stories were so distorted by their intermingling with the Jeffers narratives as to become unrecognizable. In the course of all this, the genuine flavor of the region was overlooked and, in time, forgotten. This was largely because people assumed that the Jeffers narratives were the equivalent of regional history, and felt they did not need to delve further. Outsiders were regarded with suspicion on the Coast, however, and it is doubtful that they could have penetrated the veil that hid its real life even if they had attempted it.

With the coming of the highway, this entire way of life came to an abrupt end. The winding wagon road built by settlers in 1881, that started below Carmel and ended at Post's ranch in the Big Sur some 30 miles to the south (as the crow files), was abandoned along with the Coast trail that connected Post's ranch with Hearst's castle at San Simeon, another 100 miles to the south along the mountain tops. Horses and spring-wagons began to go. Modern improvements came in gradually but steadily, and by the 1950s most of the remaining old ranch houses had running water, butane gas and modern plumbing. And, on some Coast ranches, the jeep had, to some extent, supplanted the horse. But as Sherle Patterson Bodrero of the Sousa clan at Garapata said, "The jeep can never *really* replace the horse."

Our family had been the first on the Coast to install modern plumbing; this was when my parents bought the ranch at Mill Creek in 1919; and curious neighbors came by on horseback to inspect our bathroom which they had never seen before outside the pages of the Montgomery Ward catalogue. Down Coast women began to plague their husbands to install running water like that at the Sharpe ranch so they wouldn't have to haul it in from the spring or the creek bucket by bucket. Patent toilets did not exist on the Coast in pre-highway days except at Rainbow Lodge and Pfeiffer's Resort. Florence Pfeiffer had a hard time getting her husband to consent to it, however. Johnny Pfeiffer was against these modern inventions. Finally, with the help of a friendly doctor, she wangled mandatory consent. She asked the doctor to report to the Board of Health at Salinas that conditions at the Pfeiffer place were unsanitary and that patent toilets had to be installed.

"I was much amused," Florence Pfeiffer reported in her journal, "to find the following year my husband boasting of the fine modern accommodations to be found at Pfeiffer's Resort. He never knew he had been worked for his consent in this matter."

Some of the old-timers, such as the Posts, opened tourists resorts along the highway; others sold their land and moved out. Places like Rainbow Lodge, Hoffman's Camp in the Palo Colorado and Camp Idlewild in the Little Sur became things of the past. We moved our business to the Stone House, changing its name to Bixby Inn, but here there were no cabins or campsites as there had been at Rainbow Lodge; only sandwiches, salad, chili beans, coffee, tea, beer, pie, cake, and a grandiose view.

"Don't you ever get lonely down here?" the tourists asked us. We got tired of making the same old answer, so my inventive mother developed a stock reply, "Well, maybe we would if only there weren't so many people around." Another thing they asked was where we got our chili beans. It was too boring to tell them the obvious truth, that we made them ourselves, so Mother said there was a little old Indian lady up at the top of the mountain. She'd point out the window at Bixby Mountain. "Do you see that mountain up there? Well, every morning the old Indian lady fills baskets with chili beans and ties them to the sides of her horse and comes down the trail with them at dawn. She gets here around breakfast time. So we have beans for breakfast."

The tourists fell for this as well as my mother's other vivid, spontaneously conceived tales, hook, line and sinker.

The Posts of Rancho Sierra del Mar were also plagued with witless questions. One of them was, "Is there any way to get off this road?"

"Why yes," the Posts replied, "Just drive straight off the cliff."

We began to realize that the old way of life was really gone when we saw that even Robinson Jeffers was forgotten.

Mother had a beautiful picture of Jeffers hanging on the redwood wall next to the door leading out to the observation porch. He had inscribed it to her, mentioning Bixby Landing, the locale of *Thurso's Landing*.

"Who's that? Gary Cooper?" people asked.

When we explained that no, it was the great poet Robinson Jeffers, they looked utterly blank. *Medea* and Broadway hadn't happened yet.

There are very few people on the Coast today who remember the Sur as it was before the highway went through. Those who do are proud of their heritage and feel nostalgic about it, but it has grown so remote from the present as to seem incommunicable and even lost. Who cares for the memories of old women and old men, forgotten grandmothers and grandfathers? Into the grave all will go and their souvenirs and mementos with them.

The old landmarks are gone. An entire way of life is gone. A world is gone. How is one to convey to the living the days of the dead? Or even that they, the dead, existed in this now so curiously unhaunted place?

And yet, more and more contemporary voices arise to demand insistently, "Tell us about the Big Sur before it is too late. Tell us how it was."

This little book is written to help fill in this gap, to try to recapture or evoke the picture of a vanished world and the people who were a part of it.

I was one of those people, for I grew up in the Sur at Mill Creek (Bixby Creek.)

Even as I write this I can hear the babbling creek and the clop clop of horses' hooves as they crossed the old wooden bridge. Blown in on the wind I see John Gilkey, who in 1875 built the house we lived in, riding along the old county road on Betty Horse, his violin tucked under his arm and his wavy auburn beard and long auburn hair flowing out behind him, saying, "This is a free life, not crowded..."

I never saw John Gilkey. He was before my time. But the memory of him hovered over the land, especially at Mill Creek where he had built his first home in this then formidable wilderness. His daughters were still alive when I was a child, and one of them, Lizzie Post, the wife of Joe Post of Big Sur, often stopped by our place for a soft drink or some coffee on her way to town. I was there, in our country store, when she came by with her new, big, handsome dark stallion and said to my mother, "That horse is going to kill me one day."

"Then why don't you get rid of it?" Mother asked.

"No," said Lizzie Gilkey Post firmly, and without further explanation.

The whole Coast was stunned when Lizzie Post was found dead in Terrace Creek. Her stallion had slipped on the rock, falling backwards on Lizzie and breaking her neck. A sad end for a courageous and much admired woman who was also a top-notch rider and cattle woman.

***

These ghosts and many others crowd the mind, seeming to skirt over the landscape like a mist, a scarf of fog. They melt at the edges into sunlight and sea foam and stern cliffs of granite. In a way, however, they seem very thin and insubstantial in comparison to the land itself, which has a powerful presence and appears to have triumphed over its human inhabitants. So few relics of the past remain that it is almost uncanny, as though a giant hand had wiped them out.

There is undeniably something peculiar about the Sur, something strange and uncommon. There is a force here, a definite presence; and it has a stirring, compelling quality like a storm wind or a flight of wild geese overhead; yet many people are frightened of it if they get too close. Some believe it is dark, sinister and dangerous and talk of unfriendly nature spirits.

John Steinbeck's mother, who taught school at Big Sur before the turn of the century, reported seeing "little dark people" who stood about three feet high and clustered against the canyon walls and in the depths of the redwood forests. I, too, once saw these little dark people at Mill Creek long before I ever heard of them from Robinson Jeffers. They did not seem to me to be sinister, however; they were simply *there*. One had to know the Coast, to actually live there and be a part of it, to get on friendly terms with it.

As a child I never went into a wood alone without first, inwardly, asking permission to enter and waiting for an answer, and if I picked a flower or plant I also asked permission of the plant and waited until I felt I had received it. I heard later that the American Indians did this. I believe now that living in such a place brings out the Indian spirit within one — spirits that seemed to linger there.

Although the highway has brought the outside world into the Sur, it has, at the same time, served to veil it further; for in wagon-road days one wandered in and out of every redwood canyon on the long, all-day trip from Carmel to Big Sur. One had a chance to get the feeling of the place. The highway, on the other hand, keeps to the spectacular sea-cliffs and the hidden, mysterious world that was once the heart of the Sur Coast has become invisible. It is possible to visit a portion of it, however, by taking the old road which still exists between Bixby Creek Bridge and the Molera ranch (Andrew Molera State Park) at Big Sur river mouth, and along it there remain the signs that were placed there in the early 1900s when automobiles began to appear, signs such as "Slow, Blow Horn, Go down in Second Gear," etc. There are perhaps 10 or 20 inhabitants at the most in this area where, once upon a time, there were hundreds, possibly more.

Curiously enough — or is it curious? — the only real ghosts are the Indians, the Indians who for so many centuries made their homes here before the white man came. They seem to have in some way commingled with the force of the land and to continue to be felt by those who are sensitive to them.

The Indians who lived on this Coast were the Rumsen and Esselen, two unrelated tribes who did not speak each other's language and could communicate only by sign language. Indeed, their languages were not branch languages, but sprang from two distinctly separate linguistic stocks. They had less in common than English has with Sanskrit, for they lacked similar roots. Rumsen territory (they were also called Carmelenyos) stretched from Carmel to the Little Sur; whereas Esselen territory (their true tribal name was Mukni) reached from Little Sur to Lucia.[1] Their territories also stretched inland, across the Santa Lucia mountains, into Carmel Valley. The Rumsen inhabited the lower reaches of the Carmel Valley, the Esselen the upper — and Tassajara Hot Springs, now the Zen Mountain Center, was their stronghold. Although they were unrelated and, in fact, were enemies, they lived very similar lives in the wilderness. They dwelt in huts of brush and tule in *rancherias*, the Spanish word for villages, which they moved from time to time for sanitary reasons. They were seminomadic, as they migrated back and forth between the Coast and the valley according to the season. Acorns were the staple of their diet, so during the acorn season all went inland to gather them. Otherwise they lived on shell fish, especially abalone, which was dried and stored in skin bags like venison, and on wild game such as deer, rabbit, quail, doves, etc. In addition to abalone, they ate mussels, limpets, and sea fish as well as fresh water fish including salmon and steelhead. Their bows were said to be the best in the world, better than the European bows of which the most superior were the English; their arrow heads and spearheads were of flint, traded with the Tulare Indians; and they dressed, for the most part, sparsely, the women wearing grass aprons, the men naked except in the winter.

---

[1] Lately the anthropologists have come to theorize that the entire coast below Carmel was Esselen (Mukni) territory and that the Rumsen were confined to the lower Carmel Valley and Carmel.

It was not true, as the Franciscan fathers believed, that they had no religion, but little is known about it save for their gatherings at Pico Blanco for sacred ceremonies at the time of the equinoxes. The sun had a place in their symbology and they had a legend that they came from the North after some kind of catastrophe. Anthropologists, such as Dr. A.L. Kroeber, believed that they were the remains of a once much larger tribe which had occupied much of California.

The Esselens and Rumsens were bitter enemies. They often fought — but these were mock battles in which no one was killed or even injured. They simply stood and threw stones at each other, being careful to miss. When they ran out of stones, the fight stopped. One of the reasons the incoming Americans looked down on the native California Indians was that they were so peaceful and seldom fought; consequently they referred to them as "Diggers."

These native peoples who were, in any case, not very numerous (it is estimated that there were only 500 to 1000 Esselens at the time the Spanish arrived in 1770), gradually disappeared into Carmel Mission where they died of white man's diseases to which they had never previously been exposed, as well as of malnutrition and homesickness. (The gruel they ate at the Mission along with pinole did not take the place of the wild game and fish they were accustomed to.) They also died of homesickness. Torn from their free lives in the wilderness they were miserable and could not adapt to what to them was a life of darkness and imprisonment. Runaways were severely punished, usually captured by Spanish soldiers and brought back in chains, then flogged. Many, however, were devoted to Father Serra and freely and happily adapted themselves to Christianity; but others did not and forever pined for their free life in the wide Coast mountains.

As only a handful of Indians were left after the secularization of the California Missions in 1834 by the Mexican government, they have been somewhat neglected in this story. But, in a very definite sense, their ghosts — or the feeling of their presences — haunt the place to this day.

Carmel Mission, the final resting place of all the local Rumsen and Esselen Indians of Coast and Valley. Only a handful were left after Mission secularization in 1834. —Ink drawing by author

Having grown up as I did, a solitary child in a lonely canyon, except for a brother four years younger, I was not only close to the land but to its history — Indian, Spanish, Mexican, American — and it could be said that the land of my childhood was a land of walking ghosts — or so I interpret it now when everyone is dead and I am one of the few remaining heirs to its recollections.

The Big Sur coastline. —from the author's collection

William Brainard Post, the Connecticut Yankee sailor boy who had landed at Monterey at the age of 13 and was the first to settle on the Sur coast in 1859.

—Collection of Wiliam Post III

II.

The Post Family Saga

Frank Post was an excellent raconteur. He remembered much about the Indians and seemed eager to talk about them. The thing that impressed me on that first visit was that his memories swept clear back to pre-Spanish days.

I n the summer of 1946 I went down to Big Sur on the Greyhound bus and rented the Deetjen Barn for $50 a month. The war was over. I had returned from duty with the American Red Cross and was living with my mother in fogbound Carmel, somewhat at loose ends between jobs on a newspaper and a magazine. It occured to me it might be a good idea to write a book about the Sur as it had been in pre-highway days — an idea which had long been brewing in my mind but had been forgotten during the hectic and self-sacrificing war years.

We had left the ranch, or rather the inn, at Bixby Creek after Pearl Harbor because the road was closed. My brother, "Beans," (I called him Willy) who was a sculptor, a cartoonist, and an artist who aimed to become an architect, had joined the Air Corps and been killed in 1944 as first pilot of a B-24 bomber over Lake Constance, Germany. We had no fighter protection that day; we lost 63 bombers, the heaviest loss in the war.

My mother and I did not have the heart to return to the Coast and Bixby Inn without him. His sculpture studio, a primitive one-room cabin, stood lonely and deserted on Bixby Landing with the wind howling around it and the seagulls flying. Later Frida Sharpe was to make it her place of residence and turn it into a real home, but at this particular time neither of us could even visit the old property. It still hurt too much. And, too, vandals had broken into the old restaurant, stealing not only our furniture and stove but the toilets, breaking the windows on our spectacular observation porch with its view to the south of the bridge and beach below and of Hurricane Point and the coast mountains towards Point Sur Lighthouse.

My father was no longer with us. His ill-temper and his drinking had become too much to endure, so the family divorce occurred in 1938, and he had remarried and was living in Hollywood.

Why Big Sur? For one thing it was different from the world I had grown up in on the northern part of the Coast. Although we had known the Big Sur folk, we had not known them intimately as we did our neighbors who lived closer to us — such as the Souzas at Garapata, the Brazils on Serra Hill, the Grimes at Palo Colorado (and earlier the Trotters), and the Smith family at Rocky Creek which was only a mile away. The Hogues had left Bixby Mountain just prior to the war, and so had Charlie and Alta Bixby Gregg — or rather they went just after the war started.

The distances were long in wagon-road days and although this had changed after the highway went through, the Big Sur and its annals were pretty much virgin territory as far as I was concerned. I wanted to know all about it. I had often visited Dr. Jaime de Angulo at his ranch before the war, with my mother and brother; also various artists such as Jean "Yanko" Varda (patronized by the Lathrop Browns), but still I was not well acquainted with the old-timer Post and Pfeiffer families even though I had gone to school with Mary and Bill Post, and with Frank Trotter (a Pfeiffer descendant) who was just my age.

Florence Swetnam Pfeiffer was dead. I remembered her from my childhood, bowing rather stiffly to us as she stopped at Rainbow Lodge en route to town on her yearly trek via mailstage. She wore a stovepipe headdress and appeared to regard us rather haughtily, for we were in those days newcomers, not real Down Coasters. We ourselves later grew to be very snobbish.

Esther Pfeiffer Ewoldsen was kind enough to lend me her mother's journal on the life of John Peiffer and the Pfeiffer family, and she has written many wonderful articles about early life in the Big Sur. She has not, as yet, written a book about it. But maybe she will when she has time away from her extensive gardening.

It was obvious after World War II that the ranks were thinning out: that the old-timers were getting older and fewer, and that the time would soon be coming when it would be too late to collect their histories. Already many of the people I had known as a child had disappeared, including West Smith of Westmere, Eula Draper of the Souza ranch, Sam Trotter, Harvey Abbot (an old bachelor who lived on Serra Hill), and Captain and Mrs. Tompkins. The same would soon be true of the Posts, the Harlans, the Danis, and Dr. Jaime de Angulo down in the Big Sur on Partington Ridge. Artists and writers were beginning to settle in and would soon take over. Hence my summer at the Deetjen barn from which I made long treks on foot (I had no car) to various ranches, many of them on top of steep mountain ridges, to see such people as Miss Lulu May Harlan at the Harlan Ranch and Dr. Jaime de Angulo and Sam Hopkins on Partington — to interview the few who could still remember the way things were once upon a time.

Some, such as Miss Lulu May Harlan, could remember events that occurred during her childhood in the late 1880s. She brought it very close. Time seemed to disappear.

In the end, I travelled much farther than the Big Sur to catch up on things past. I went to Carmel Mission, to Salinas and the County Records office, to King City (in search of an Esselen Indian named Tontas, but I never found him), to the Carmel Valley to see John B.R. Cooper III, grandson of the old sea captain, and everywhere on the Monterey Peninsula even remotely related to the history of the Sur. I found Josie Simoneau Fussell, the daughter of Jules Simoneau who had owned the famed Bohemian restaurant frequented by Robert Louis Stevenson and other notables in early-day Monterey; she had once occupied our ranch-house (which her husband bought from John Gilkey) and from her I learned much about Stevenson as well as the coast during the pioneer era, especially in limekiln days. I also had the great luck to find Amy Melissa Gilkey Miller in Monterey, the daughter of John

Gilkey who had built our ranch-house. I was interviewing, interviewing, interviewing, and reading musty old documents, including land deeds, transfers of title, journals, diaries, wedding certificates and death cerfiticates. It was like being engaged upon a treasure hunt or playing detective. And, of course, it all meant a lot to me personally since I had my own memories to draw upon, and felt attached to the Big Sur folk who had always been a part of my life.

The story inevitably begins with the Indians and the Spaniards who left rather more than a ghostly imprint upon the land. For the wild, primitive, precipitous, bear-infested region along the edge of the steep Santa Lucias into which American settlers poured in the 1870s and '80s was by no means untouched. During the years in which it was gradually being depleted of its native Indian populace (conversion was very slow at first), it had been under Spanish rule; then, from 1822 on, Mexican. The Spanish had strangely dreaded it, however, and avoided it with almost superstitious horror. They called it the Sur, Sur being the Spanish word for South, but this was not intended to be a name, only a geographic description.

They named one of its rivers *El Rio Grande del Sur*, the Big River of the South, and another *El Rio Chiquito del Sur*, the Little River of the South. Other Spanish place names were *Garapata*, or Woodtick, *San Jose* creek (for St. Joseph), and *Palo Colorado* or Tall Red Tree. Later the names *El Rio Grande del Sur* and *El Rio Chiquito del Sur* were contracted into the bastard English-Spanish version Big Sur and Little Sur. (Early settlers called the Little Sur Little River.)

For the most part, the Spaniards left the Coast severely alone except for expeditions to capture runaway Mission Indians or to hunt ferocious grizzly bears for Monterey's famous bear and bull fights. Possibly they were influenced by the vivid account of the terrible hardships experienced by Governor Gaspar de Portolá of Baja California and his men in 1769 when he attempted to explore the terrible Santa Lucia mountains in his fruitless search for Monterey Bay. Those on the expedition had a dreadful experience in the Santa Lucias north of San Simeon and several contracted scurvy. Early mariners too, such as Cermeno, had given awe-inspiring accounts of this fearsome region whose mountains were described as the most formidable on the entire Pacific coast. They rose relentlessly and abruptly from the sea without pause, bounded by vertical cliffs of granite; and there were very few, if any, landing places. The mountains looked peculiar, sawed off, almost unnatural, and they were indeed the tops of a great mountain range which in Jurassic times had risen to 26,000 feet above sea-level. Then, in recent times (geologically speaking) they had risen to their present height, averaging around 3,000 feet with inland peaks shooting up to over 6,000 feet; they had comprised the Santa Lucia Island which stood far from the continental shoreline. The nearest land had been at Fresno. Water lay between it and the island. Then, gradually, over a period of centuries, the water had filled up with sediment and the Santa Lucia Island became attached to the continent.

During the Mexican period, following the end of the Wars of Independence in 1822, the situation, insofar as the loneliness of the coast was concerned, began to change. Two land grants were given out, one to Marcellino Escobar, the *San Jose y Sur Chiquito* grant; the other to Governor Juan B. Alvarado, the *El Sur Rancho*. The latter consisted of two Spanish leagues, or about 8,000 acres. Nothing much was done with them in the beginning. Marcellino Escobar lost his holdings in a dice game with ten soldiers from the Presidio of Monterey. One of the soldiers, Jose Castro, bought the others out, and in the years that followed sold the same piece of land repeatedly to various comers whenever he ran out of money. This legal confusion had to be straightened out by litigation in the 1880s and many lost their land entirely since they had never had clear title. Governor Alvarado, whatever his original intentions may have been, did nothing whatever with *El Sur* but in the 1830s

Capt. Juan Bautista Rogers Cooper who arrived in California in 1823 and commanded the sea otter trade in partnership with Governor Arguello; later established El Sur Rancho as a cattle ranch and smuggling base.   — Collection of Amelie Elkinton

or 1840s gave or sold it to his uncle, Captain Juan Bautista Rogers Cooper.

Captain Cooper was called Juan el Manco, or John the Maimed, because he had a maimed left hand. Originally an Englishman born in the Channel Islands, he had come to America as a boy with his widowed mother who married a man named Larkin in New England, and Thomas Larkin, the first American consul to Monterey, was his half-brother. Cooper had sold his vessel, *The Rover*, to Governor Arquello and went into partnership with him in the sea otter hunting business. This was in 1823. His vessel, in fact, was the only one belonging to the newly created Mexican province. Cooper commanded the highly lucrative sea otter trade (California had made a deal with the Russians at Fort Ross, on account of foreign hunters invading their waters) until 1841 when the sea otters were declared extinct. Following the Gold Rush, Cooper lost his extensive landholdings all over the State of California to squatters except for his Castroville ranch and the one at *El Sur*. In the 1850s, he was hard put to make a living so he decided to become a smuggler. Since the Americans had taken over, the customs duty was inordinately high at Monterey. *El Sur Rancho* provided an ideal base for operations. Cargos from China or the Sandwich Islands could be landed there and anchored offshore to be transferred to little boats to go into the mouth of the Big Sur river. Then Cooper ran the contraband into Monterey on horseback, on the coast trail which he had built for this express purpose. As a screen for these illicit activities, he imported cattle from Guernsey, one of the Channel Islands, and cross-bred them, thus developing the best breeding stock in all of California. His title to *El Sur Rancho* was not confirmed until 1855, although he had been using it for nearly twenty years — possibly because the Americans had taken California and the laws were changing.

It was through Captain Cooper and *El Sur Rancho* that Spanish culture reached the Sur and became dominant in the American period that followed. He had married the beautiful Doña Encarnacion de Vallejo, a member of one of the most prominent families in the Spanish province, and although she never visited *El Sur* all the vaqueros were Spanish, Mexican or Indian and spoke nothing but Spanish. Therefore Spanish was the language spoken when the first settlers arrived during the American period and they were forced to become bi-lingual. The *varsoviana*, brought to Alta California from Mexico City in the 18th century, became the traditional dance not only in Monterey, the capital of the province, but in the Sur, and was still being danced at annual round-ups and barbecues as recently as the 1950s. Above all, the Spanish pattern of hospitality, instituted by Captain Cooper and continued by his son, John B.H. Cooper, became the way of the Coast. It was unthinkable to charge a traveller for food and lodging or feed for his horses. Everyone was welcome whether stranger, friend or outcast. John Cooper II, who had inherited the Little Sur portion of the ranch, always kept a supply of gold coins in a bowl on a dresser as a protection again bandits. Who would steal what they could have without even asking? John Cooper III, whom I met when he was in his 80s and living in the Carmel Valley, told me that his father was very much afraid of brigands, of which there were many in the Sur duing the latter part of the 19th century.

***

The Indian influence was less obvious than the Spanish, yet it was strongly felt. Although no Esselens or Rumsens had returned to the Sur, early settlers were constantly being reminded of them through various relics and artifacts, such as the post-holes of their houses. Flint arrowheads were found scattered on the ridges; there were kitchen middens near

The old J.B.H. Cooper barn next to the vanished house on Cooper Hill in the Little Sur (half of the El Sur Rancho grant). The house, not seen in this picture, boasted 6 bathtubs.
— Photograph by Brett Weston

creeks and at the mouths of canyons there were shell mounds on the cliffs; and occasionally skeletons, buried in the traditional knee to chest or fetal position, were turned up in the spring ploughing. I once found a beautiful stone scraper, a pale green stone shaped like a crescent moon with a chipped sharp cutting edge, in a shell-mound at our beach; and my father found the skull of a grizzly bear with a spearhead embedded in it up the creek in a thicket where the beast had evidently crawled off to die.

To me it seemed that the Indian, in a silent, invisible fashion, haunted the land. It was as though the hundreds, nay thousands of dead had somehow become a part of it. I remember that as a small child I never took a walk through the forests without feeling that Indians walked before me on the trail, and that if I were quick and quiet — I might just stray upon one, carrying his bow and arrow or fishing for trout, salmon, or steelhead. I practiced walking like an Indian, making no sound, disturbing not a single cracking leaf. Down at the beach, where the Indians used to gather shellfish and make bonfires, their bronzed faces seemed still to linger, their voices still to be heard against the seawind — a feeling which Robinson Jeffers often reflected in his verse (e.g., "Human Hands" — a short poem about the imprint or paintings of hands in a cave at Tassajara Hot Springs which was the heart of Esselen territory). Jeffers, like myself, felt very close to the spirit of the Indians and it is said that he had a strain of native American blood — a fact which his face would seem to confirm. (I myself have a little American Indian blood; Huron, Penabscot, Susquehanna and Assiniboin — but in addition I have every type of European ancestry and might be described as typical American goulash).

I first met the older generation of the Post family, the first Americans to settle on the coast below Carmel, in 1946 — in my summer at the Deetjen barn. These were Charles Francis Post and Joseph William Post, generally referred to by the Big Sur folk as Uncle Frank and Uncle Joe. They were both men in their 80s. Their father was William Brianard Post, a

Connecticut Yankee sailor, and their mother had been a Rumsen Indian from the Carmel Valley named Anselma Onesimo. And so Uncle Joe and Uncle Frank were half Indian, and Uncle Frank was the one who remembered everything vividly, including the stories he had heard as a little boy about his Indian ancestors who had survived the Mission system. It was his cousin, Isabel Meadows, the daughter of his aunt Loretta Meadows, who had given information about her tribe, the Rumsens or Carmelenyo, to the Smithsonian Institute.

Charles Francis Post (above), born at Soberanes Creek March 1, 1859, the first child to be born in the Sur during the American period. With his wife, née Annie Pate, of Little Sur. At Loma Vista Inn. — Courtesy of Steve Yaeger

I first went to see Joe Post who lived in the original Post ranchhouse built in 1877 at the top of the hill overlooking the Big Sur River Valley. He was a handsome man with true old world courtesy. But after a few words he directed me to his brother, Frank.

"Frank can tell you everything you want to know. He's the historian of the family," he said. "Just ask him. My memory isn't so sharp now."

He was 84 years old that year, and his older brother, Frank, was 87.

Joseph W. Post, Frank's younger brother born at Soberanes Creek in 1862. He and his wife Lizzy (Elizabeth Gilkey Post), lived in the old family ranch house on the hill beyond Big Sur.
—Collection of William Post III

Frank Post lived down the hill at Loma Vista Inn which he owned in partnership with his daugher, Alice, and her husband, Steve Yaeger. His wife, Annie, was still alive; she had been born Annie Pate of the Little Sur. So I walked down the hill and found Uncle Frank sitting on a log outside the begonia gardens. He was wearing overalls and had a hat pulled down low over his eyes; he had a very bronzed face, a hooked nose. He looked completely Indian. He was at first so silent as to cause me to feel shy, even tongue-tied. How can I get him to talk? I had walked five miles to see him from the Deetjen barn and now that I was there I didn't know where to begin or how. I offered him a beer. He declined.

"Indians don't drink beer," he said laconically.

In desperation I decided to get bold. I decided to pretend I felt no shyness and to be a natural-born chatter-box. (More than once I had to use this same technique when talking to Robinson Jeffers unless Una was there to rescue us.) And very soon the seemingly silent Uncle Frank was launched on tales. He would start out stutteringly, saying, "And-a And-a And-a..." and then an account would begin.

Eddie Post with his parents—Annie and Frank Post of Loma Vista Inn, Big Sur.. —Collection of Steve Yaeger

Frank Post was an excellent raconteur. He remembered much about the Indians and seemed eager to talk about them. The thing that impressed me on that first visit was that his memories swept clear back to pre-Spanish days. How extraordinary! When he was born in 1859, his great-great-great-grandmother was still alive and she was 130 years old—"as nearly as we could calculate." As a little boy, Frank had lived with his family at Soberanes Creek, not far below Carmel and Point Lobos, and his mother's relatives, the Onesimos and Meadows, lived in the Carmel Valley which was no great distance. They visited frequently, and he told me that the face of his great-great-great grandmother "was wrinkled like an old apple," and "she walked bent over with the aid of a stick."

One time, when she was a young woman, a bear had tried to get into her family

Alice Post Yaeger at Loma Vista Inn — daughter of Frank Post
—Collection of Steve Yaeger

brush-hut, and someone said, "Let's take a stick from the fire and burn his paw." "No, no," someone else cried. "That would only infuriate him and he would be sure to get us." So they decided to just stay quiet and keep their thoughts quiet, so that the bear would not feel their fear and agitation. After a while, the bear went away.

She had been a woman of about 39 or 40 when Father Serra built his Mission at the mouth of Carmel River in 1771, so she had probably been born around 1730. Her memories went back to the days when no one had ever seen a white man, but strange ships with billowing white sails, looking like birds, had been passing along the coast for two centuries or more — a familiar mystery. It was said that one of these strange ships had landed at Monterey and that bearded men, tall, with pale faces and wearing extraordinary clothing, had come ashore and planted a cross upon a hill. Not everyone believed this; it was like tales of flying saucers today. No further landings had occurred, but the strange, bird-like ships, ever greater in number, continued to pass along the shores. By 1769, when the Portola expedition appeared on foot, it is doubtful if the Indians were particularly surprised or gave them much thought. On the other hand, their actual appearance may have been a great shock.

But it was not long before the establishment of a colony and Presidio at Monterey in 1770 and the Mission at Carmel a year later, changed all this and brought an end to the peaceful and abundant life the Indians had known in the wilderness. Frank Post's great-great-great- grandmother was among those converted to Christianity, and taken to the Mission until the Missions were secularized by the Mexican government in 1834. She was one of the very, very few survivors of what had been, for the Indians, the equivalent of the Holocaust.

It was in 1848 that a lad named Boy Bill Post turned up in Monterey, left off by a man o'war, after having been stranded at La Paz months earlier. He was only 13 years old. A native of Connecticut, he was the son of a retired sea captain and his ancestors had come to America on the Mayflower. From the time he was a small boy he had been crazy about the sea and wanted to follow in his father's footsteps.

"Dad's mother gave him a watch his father used to carry to sea," Frank Post related. "It was of English make. The works ran on little chains. He always wanted it covered with silver. The jeweler thought it ought to have a gold case but Father insisted on silver."

"Father tried to sign on a vessel at Boston, but it was full-handed," Uncle Frank continued. "It later disappeared. Then two whalers came in, *The Brooklyn* and the *Hibernia*. He signed on *The Brooklyn* as a cabin-boy, being too young to go before the mast. He sailed the Atlantic — to Scotland, the Azores Islands, the Cape of Good Hope, Australia, New Zealand, the South Sea Islands, Honolulu, the Bering Sea, then back to Lower California. At Magdalena Bay he got a permit to go ashore and a friend was along with him. He came to an old ranchhouse where the two boys stayed overnight. The next morning they found that the vessel was gone. A wind had come up and it had gone around a bend in a point. Father returned to the ranch, not having found the vessel, and stayed there until he had no shoes left on his feet. Either he had to hike overland, be eaten by coyotes, die of thirst, or get on another ship."

Boy Bill Post and his friend walked barefooted to La Paz.

"They got a ship at La Paz," Frank Post went on. "It was a government vessel with guns and it took them aboard. They signed articles as able seamen. But the proviso was that they had to be left off at the first port in Alta California. The ship was called *The Mizzen Top* and San Francisco was their destination, At that time San Francisco was called Yerba Buena. It was a mere village in the sand-hills. As it turned out, Father was dumped off at the beach at Monterey. He was penniless. But he could read and write Spanish. He spent his first night in Monterey at the old brickhouse near the Wharf. This was in March, 1848. He fished in the bay with an old fisherman and peddled fish in town for 'four bits' or a dollar. He was living from day to day. The gold rush started in 1849. He left for the gold fields and panned for nuggets. He returned to Monterey as poor as when he had left."

When Post got back to Monterey he found it almost a ghost town, for everyone had left for the gold fields at the same time he did. The once glittering Spanish capital had been moved from Monterey to Sacramento soon after gold was discovered at Sutter's Fort. In 1858 he married Anselmo Onesimo, a lovely Rumsen Indian girl from the Carmel Valley. Her sister, Loretta, was also married to a white man named Roy Meadows. The Meadows had a farm in the Valley, but Post, because of his background at sea, wanted to settle on the coast where he would be in sight of it. He found a piece of land at Soberanes Creek on the old *San Jose y Sur Chiquito* grant and decided it was a good place to raise cattle. There was plenty of grazing in the hills above. It was true that this was grizzly bear country but so was the rest of California; Post did not know that these bears were much more dangerous and powerful than other American bears.

Mrs. Post was expecting a baby when they moved down to Soberanes and Post immediately went to work building a cabin.

"At Soberanes, Dad was building a hut in the creek bottom," Frank Post related. "He hadn't quite finished the roof. Rain was coming and I was expected. Dad hurried to finish the roof that day. Sure enough, I was born — under a roof."

Post had barely nailed the last hand-split shake in place when the baby was born, ushered in on a March gale from the south. The date was March 1, 1859 and the child was named Charles Francis Post. He was the first baby to be born in the Sur during the American period. In 1862, his brother Joseph W. Post was born, and later two sisters, Mary and Ellen.

Mrs. Post, being Indian, had a habit of wandering off into the wilderness, sometimes to be gone two or three days at a time. The family was used to it and never worried.

But one night, when little Frank was only four years old, a strange thing happened. A terrible storm had come up and and the child could not get to sleep. He kept worrying about his mother, who had gone off on one of her treks. Then a light appeared in the little boy's room. It grew very bright and seemed to beckon him. He got out of bed and followed the light. The light led him outdoors and up a steep trail. He followed it until he came almost to the top of the ridge. There the light flared up and then went out. He found his mother pinioned under a tree which had fallen on her, blown down by the storm. She was uninjured but could not get free without help. With seemingly superhuman strength, the four-year-old was able to lift the tree from the body of his mother just enough to let her get out, and together they walked down the trail to the house as the storm raged on.

When old Frank Post told me this tale, tears came to his eyes. Over 80 years later, he was still deeply moved by it.

Many of Uncle Frank's tales of life at Soberanes Creek had to do with grizzly bears. The coast grizzly was another breed altogether from those found elsewhere in California or anywhere in America. They were huge, heavy, and extremely dangerous; they attacked without provocation and made life very hazardous for early settlers as well as for the Indians who had preceded them. Finally, settlers learned that if they tied a ball of fat containing poison in the branches of an oak tree, the bear would eat it and die. However, there were still bears left to plague the settlers and their livestock. The last bear killed on the coast was at *El Sur Rancho* in 1881. A famous hunter named Jacobo Escobar came down from Monterey and shot him and collected a reward of $50. The bear weighed 1,500 pounds, could travel 45 miles per hour, and had a foot-spread of 16 inches.

One day Post went out hunting deer in the mountains with Jonathan Wright, the hired man, and ran into a bear unexpectedly.

"Father had a mule," Frank Post told me, "and he could shoot from the saddle. The mule wouldn't move. On his way back that day he heard a noise. At the time they used muzzle loaders. You had to pour the powder down the barrel, use cloth and a ramrod, then put the cap on. The noise turned out to be a bear and the bear was coming for him. Father could see his white teeth. He started the mule up, dodging the limbs of oaks but the bear was gaining. Father took a shot at the bear and struck the ground. The bear took off. Father lost his speech for a while. Then he climbed up an oak tree and sat there, afraid to come down. He thought the bear might come back. He discovered that his gun was still loaded but the wiping stick had been shot out. Evidently the wiping stick had hit the bear in the face and frightened him. Father got down from the tree. Round about downhill he found the mule with his forward leg through the bridle reins. He got on the mule and went home. Johathan Wright asked him, 'Where's the deer?' Father couldn't answer. He had lost his speech. Finally he told the story at dinnertime. What had happened was that the mule jumped over a hole and Father had fallen into the hole. The bear didn't see him because the wiping stick had struck him across the face. Father was afraid of bears after that.'"

Uncle Frank had many more bear stories to tell, the most

interesting of which was about the bear with a cub who grabbed Post's dog, Tige, and broke his jaw, shaking him madly. W.B. Post took a shot at the bear and hit her in a vital spot. She didn't die immediately, however. "She broke brush and she coughed, she broke brush and she coughed. Finally she fell dead on the trail." This was down in the willows along the creek not far from the cabin at Soberanes. The cub ran off into the wilderness.

Post tied up Tige's jaw with a splint and rags, and they hand-fed him for over six months until he was well again.

The coast was lonely in those early days at Soberanes with no neighbors, but once a month or so they would hear the thundering of horses' hooves as the vaqueros, fifty strong, came up from *El Sur Rancho* on the coast trail, each carrying two leather saddlebags filled with contraband. There were 100 leather saddlebags altogether. Peeking out from the hut in the creek bottom at night, the Post children could sometimes catch a glimpse of the riders when the moon was full. Most of the contraband was smuggled at night in order to evade the sharp eyes of the watchful Customs officers at Monterey. Cooper was the one who had built the coast trail in the 1830s or 1840s, long before the Posts moved to Soberanes, as a smuggler's trail. Formerly there had been nothing but deer trails after the Indian trails grew over.

The only other inhabitant of the Sur at this time was a hermit named George Davis who lived in the Big Sur Valley. But in 1862, the year Frank's little brother Joseph W. Post was born, a Portuguese whaling station was established at Point Lobos, a few miles north of Soberanes. The Azores Islanders who worked there built themselves a village with pigs, chickens, and even flower gardens, but it was not a very pleasant place to live on account of the stench of rotting whale carcasses. The Point Lobos whaling station with its whaler's knoll (which was the original model of Spyglass Mountain in

Robert Louis Stevenson's *Treasure Island*) was a branch of the main whaling station at Monterey.

Once a week a priest went down to Point Lobos to say Mass. In 1877, another branch whaling station was established at Point Sur (later the site of Point Sur Lighthouse), but it was abandoned in 1880. Following the decline of the whaling industry, several of the Azores Islanders settled on the coast and started raising cattle, among them the Victorines, the Souzas (also spelled Soyzer) and the Brazils.

In 1864 there was a severe drought in California. Settlers from other parts of the country including the Salinas Valley brought their cattle to the Monterey coast to graze, and Post's cattle were starved out. He went deer hunting —there were literally thousands of deer in the hills — and sold their hides in Monterey at ten cents apiece. (Mrs. Post jerked the venison so it would not be wasted.) But this did not yield enough money to support his family, so in 1866 he sold his ranch to David Castro, the chief vaquero at *El Sur*, for $100, and moved to Castroville. His two daughters, Mary and Ellen, worked for their board and room for a family at the head of Elkhorn Slough in order to go to school.

In Castroville, Post opened a butcher shop, then he bought 200 acres of land which he planted in grain and sold the grain at 90 cents a sack. Eventually he owned a big grain warehouse in Castroville, but he missed the sea, so he got a job at Moss Landing as a wharf builder.

"Dad was a good wharf builder and he was offered a job in San Pedro," Frank Post recalled, "but he decided to return to the Big Sur instead."

He sold his grain warehouse and, after making a trip to Connecticut to visit relatives, he went down to Big Sur and bought 160 acres from Cristobal Castro in 1877. Cristobal was the father of David Castro to whom he had sold the Soberanes Place in 1866. Ironically, David had bought the Soberanes ranch in order to get his father away from town and drink. But he soon discovered that his father could easily get to town for wine, so he moved him down to Big Sur — only to discover that somehow this also was too close to town; the old man somehow slipped out and got wine. Hence the sale of the land to Post — and the Castros moved a bit farther south. But, as far as was known, Cristobal Castro managed to keep on drinking until the end of his days.

Dining room at the Pfeiffer Ranch Resort.

III.

The Homesteaders

Some settlers raised cattle, but in this steep mountain country it took 25 acres to graze a single head, therefore one had to have a lot of land to make a living through raising cattle. Others started industries such as tanbark, lumber, the making of fence posts and railway ties, limekilns, gold mines, silver mines, copper mines and the like.

It was in 1869, just three years after Post sold his place to David Castro, that the first of the American homesteaders arrived in the Big Sur. Michael Pfeiffer was of German descent and his wife, née Barbara Laque, was a native of France. Unlike Cooper and Post, Pfeiffer was not a seafaring man: he was a farmer. Soon after the Pfeiffers were married in 1858, they joined a wagon train to California. The Gold Rush was in full swing, but they were not interested in gold; they wanted land.

They first settled in Vacaville as tenant farmers. They worked hard and the farm prospered with the result that the owner raised the rent; so they moved to Tomales Bay where the same thing happened. Disgusted, they started studying maps. The Homestead Act of 1864 had opened up thousands of acres for settlement but most of the good land in California was already taken. Pfeiffer discovered that there was plenty of land open for homestead on the coast below Big Sur, beyond the reach of the Spanish grant-land which ended at the mouth of Big Sur River.

El Sur, by this time, was no longer a center of smuggling activities. Captain Cooper was getting to be an old man and had retired from the sea. Although he had built a house at *El Sur,* (later used by his daughter and son-in-law, the Eusebio Moleras) he never lived there but used it only as headquarters when on business. This was because his wife, the beautiful Doña Encarnacion de Vallejo Cooper, refused to go down there. She could not go by sea as she got seasick, and riding the rough trail for a lady of her age and station was unthinkable. The Coopers, therefore, made their home in Monterey but Cooper spent a great deal of time at *El Sur* during sea otter hunting, sailing, trading and smuggling days. *El Sur* was the last of his once vast holdings in California aside from his Castroville ranch, and after he ceased sailing he concentrated on cattle ranching. Cooper had the best breeding stock in all of California since he had imported Guernseys, Jer-

Michael and Barbara Laque Pfeiffer, the first of the homesteaders to settle in Big Sur in 1869. They chose Sycamore Canyon as their Home Place. The historic ranch house still stands near Pfeiffer Cove. — Collection of Frank Trotter.

seys, Aberdeens, and Herefords from the Channel Islands and crossbred them. But the drought of 1866 had taken its toll, and in 1869, the very same year that the courageous Pfeiffers struggled down the rough Coast trail with their stock, Cooper leased his ranch for five years to A.L. Rowntree and moved to San Francisco where he died two years later at the age of 80.

At Tomales Bay, Michael Pfeiffer heard that there was good grazing land at Pacific Valley, which was halfway between Monterey and San Luis Obispo, and in October of 1869 the Pfeiffers took a boat to Monterey with their four children, Charles, John, Julia and Mary Ellen, and their livestock.

According to the *Monterey Peninsula Guidebook* published by James Ladd Delkin it was a rough trip:

> *It was a gray, windy day when the old side wheeler Sierra Nevada pulled out from the wharf, carrying on board Michael Pfeiffer, his young wife Barbara and their four children. The housing above the paddle-wheel was used as a corral for Pfeiffer's cattle. The trip was a nightmare, waves breaking clear over the boat, while all the seasick passengers clung grimly to the rail. The*

evening of the second day the little Sierra Nevada chugged into the calm waters of Monterey; and young Mrs. Pfeiffer, too ill to stand, had somehow to get her four wan and weeping children ashore and begin to make preparations for the hard part of the journey which was still ahead of them, 40 miles of Indian trail, leading at last to Sycamore Canyon in the untouched vastness of the Big Sur.

By the time the Pfeiffers reached the Big Sur an entire week later, their cattle were thin and tired. And this part of the trip would be much worse than what they had already experienced, because from here on the trail kept to the mountain tops, far from water and shelter. And not a soul lived there to give aid in case of emergency. This was the domain of the mountain lion and the grizzly bear and the howling coyote. After crossing the river near Big Sur river mouth where the original Cooper grant land cabin stood, they followed the crest of the ridge (later called Pfeiffer Ridge) south. They could not easily have gone through the thickly timbered Big Sur River Valley with its thick underbrush and fierce grizzly bears. On the ridge the land was more open and the brush not so dense. They spotted a beach far below at the mouth of a canyon. This was later called Sycamore Cove. They turned off at Deer Ridge Canyon and camped several nights at Sycamore before deciding to rest up there for the winter. There was plenty of water and grass for the cattle and horses. Just before they came to Sycamore Canyon they lost their last 50 cent piece on the ridge which seemed somehow symbolic.

As it turned out, they never went on to Pacific Valley. They had found their Home Place — as all the early settlers called it. They arrived on October 14, 1869, and when spring came Pfeiffer started building a house. The ranch house, the first of its kind to be built on the wild Big Sur Coast, still stands, not far from the beach at Pfeiffer Cove.

The last time I visited it, it was occupied by Alvin and Kate Pfeiffer Dani. Kate was the youngest of the Pfeiffer girls, and had been born at Big Sur, along with her twin brother, Frank. Kate Dani, whose husband came from Lucia, was very proud of her flower garden and justifiably so; it contained some highly unusual items such as green roses and ferns that budded and bloomed. She also had a large collection of marine specimens, including an eight - pointed starfish. Her older sister, Mary Ellen, had been her husband's first wife and had met with a tragic death.

Alvin and Kate Dani in their later years at the old family homestead at Sycamore. Alvin Dani came from Lucia and remembered coming over Jolon pass in the snow in the 1870s.   — Collection of Frank Trotter

She committed suicide by taking strychnine when she discovered her husband was in love with Kate.

Life was not easy in the beginning for the Pfeiffers and it is worth describing, since it was typical of the lives of other pioneer homesteaders who came into the region, also into Lucia, in the 1860s and the years that followed. The account given here is a paraphrased extract from Florence Swetnam Brown Pfeiffer's journal — her own personal account of the Pfeiffer family history. She had been born in Kentucky and was already a young woman when her father, I. N. Swetnam built the redwood log home at Palo Colorado (later occupied by the Sam Trotters and the Corbett Grimes). She had first married a man named Brown, then John Pfeiffer, the second oldest of the eight Pfeiffer children. (His older brother, Charles, had migrated to Idaho, his sister Adelaide had married Sam Trotter, Julia had become Julia Burns, Frank had gone to Alaska, and Mary Ellen and Kate had both married Alvin Dani. The last four of the eight Pfeiffer children had all been born at Big Sur: Adelaide, William, Frank and Kate.) John Pfeiffer, a bachelor in his 40's when Florence married him, was the only one of the four Pfeiffer boys who stayed on permanently in the Big Sur.

Florence Swetnam Pfeiffer, wife of John Pfeiffer, who accidentally started her tourist resort in 1910 when she got angry at a man who was beating his mule with a picket. "It's your mule and you can beat it, I suppose," she said, "but from now on I charge you for food and lodging."
— Collection of Esther Pfeiffer Ewoldsen

Frank Pfeiffer born at Big Sur
—Collection of Frank Trotter

At Sycamore, grizzly bears and mountain lions preyed on the livestock. They lost two colts to lions, as well as heifers and calves. Mrs. Pfeiffer was often left alone at the ranch when Michael Pfeiffer went to town for months at a time to work for wages. Alone and unaided she raised her eight children as well as cattle, horses, sheep, goats and chickens. She fought off bears, lions, skunks, bobcats, lynxes and other predators single-handed, using her husband's muzzle-loader.   There   were   also weasels to prey on the chickens. In addition to caring for the livestock, she maintained a vegetable garden, made preserves,

carded her own wool and made it into garments. Indeed, there was nothing on the Pfeiffer ranch that the hard working and indomitable Barbara Pfeiffer did not produce. Busy from dawn until dusk, she ruled her children with a rod of iron. She had to, otherwise they could not have survived in the wilderness. Amazingly this redoubtable woman stood only five feet tall. It is said that she still commanded her sons as though they were youngsters when they were gray-headed men in their fifties.

John Pfeiffer, second eldest Pfeiffer son and the only one to remain and make his life in the Big Sur.
—Collection of Frank Trotter

In the first few years the Pfeiffers' only neighbors were the Innocentis, who were Indians. They lived about six or seven miles away, in the Big Sur redwoods. Manuel Innocenti, the chief vaquero at *El Sur* (he had taken David Castro's place) was a Chumash from Santa Barbara and his wife Francesca was a Salinan born at Mission San Antonio de Padua at Jolon. They had bought their little place from the hermit, George Davis, for $50. It had many fruit trees such as mission pear, apple, apricot, peach and even grape

Charles Pfeiffer, eldest Pfeiffer boy, who left Big Sur for Idaho but returned later in life.
—Collection of Frank Trotter

vines. Davis, an educated man, had devised his own irrigation system. But Davis had grown tired of his solitary Thoreau-like existence by the time the Innocentis turned up,

Mary Ellen Pfeiffer Dani. The eldest Pfeiffer daughter and first wife of Alvin Dani of Lucia. They lived at Pico Blanco, but Mary Ellen committed suicide on learning that her husband was in love with her younger sister, Kate.
— Collection of Frank Trotter

looking for a place to live. They had six children and there were no dwelling quarters for families at *El Sur.*

Not long after the Pfeiffers arrived at Sycamore, Francesca Innocenti walked all the way from her place in Big Sur to ask Mrs. Pfeiffer for medicine for a sick child. Barbara Pfeiffer had nothing but castor oil of which she gave a tablespoonful to Francesca Innocenti. From this time on, Mrs. Innocenti made a trip once a year to visit her "white sister." The trail was hazardous on account of grizzly bears but she kept to the open and high places as much as possible.

At a certain point in the trail, just out of sight of the Pfeiffer ranch house, she stopped and put on her shoes, which she wore only on these occasions. She always brought a gift, usually seeds.

She often talked to Mrs. Pfeiffer about her life at Mission San Antonio de Padua, but especially the times when once a year the Mission fathers permitted the Indians to return to the wilderness and roam with their tribes. This had been their one great happy annual event. But after the Mission broke up, so did the tribes — or what was left of them. They had nothing to return to, and became flotsam and jetsam on the labor market, available for

Julia Pfeiffer Burns, second eldest Pfeiffer daughter, married late but happily. Julia Pfeiffer Burns State Park bears her name.
— Collection of Frank Trotter

hire at slave wages. Many claimed that the Mexican secular authorities had been less than altruistic in ending the Mission system. It had been the intention of the Franciscans to ultimately give the land to the Indians, but the Mexican government put a stop to this and their native lands had been taken over by Spanish and Mexican grants. The few remaining Indians had no place to go.

Kate Pfeiffer Dani. The second Mrs. Alvin Dani and the youngest of the Pfeiffer children. She and Alvin lived in the old homestead at Sycamore Canyon near the Cove.
—Collection by Frank Trotter

Francesca Innocenti was lonely at Big Sur, for there were no other Indians, and Barbara Pfeiffer, her "white sister," lived seven miles away, but everything changed in 1877 when the Posts moved to Big Sur, for Mrs. Post too was an Indian. Tragically, all but one of the Innocenti children died of tuberculosis. The only one who escaped was the oldest, Juan, who succumbed to a sunstroke while climbing a mountain—probably Mount Manuel, named for his father.

"Manuel, José, Rosa and a baby all died of tuberculosis," Frank Post told me, "and the old Indian woman was left alone when her last son died. So we built a home for her in the old orchard. We promised to take care of her as long as she lived, then the lands would go to Father. My sister Mary (who later married José de la Torre) took care of her. Before she died, she said, 'This dress that I have on right now, don't let nobody take if off. Bury me in this

Kate Pfeiffer Dani with her five children —Margaret, Kathren, Albert, Stanley, and Donald.
— Collection of Frank Trotter

The Post family homestead below Big Sur built in 1877 by W.B. Post and his two sons, Frank and Joe. The wagon-road, built at the instigation of Post, ended here in 1881. The old house still stands.
— Collection of Frank Trotter

dress.' We buried her with her children, on John Pfeiffer's land. The old man, Manuel Innocenti, went crazy and died in Napa."

By an odd coincidence, Michael Pfeiffer, too, went crazy in his old age, but as he was gentle and harmless he died peacefully at home. The family thought he had probably suffered a stroke.

Mr. & Mrs. David Castro and family—Alex, Rebecca, Lorena, Minnie, Alvera, Roche, Cary Tony and Dan. Mrs. Castro, née Amadia Vasquez was first cousin to the famous bandit Tiburcio Vasquez.
—Collection of Frank Trotter

David Castro arrived in the Big Sur in 1873, spear-heading a wave of settlers who came struggling down the Coast trail from Monterey, afoot or on horseback, to settle south of Big Sur and try to make a living in these wild, precipitous hills. No one had, as yet, settled south of the Pfeiffers. Among the newcomers were Tom Slate, the Partington broth-

ers, the Anderson brothers, Bert Stevens, Phil Dolan, the McQuades, José de
la Torre, and Ed Grimes, all of whom
were to become prominent in the annals
of the Sur. At the same time, Dani and
Harlan reached Lucia from the Salinas
Valley via the Jolon Pass.

Some settlers raised cattle, but in this
steep mountain country it took 25 acres
to graze a single head, therefore one had
to have a lot of land to make a living
through raising cattle. Others started
industries such as tanbark, lumber, the
making of fence posts and railway ties,
limekilns, gold mines, silver mines,
copper mines and the like. The Harlans

Electa Dani Grimes with her
aunt and step-mother, Kate
Pfeiffer Dani. Electa married
Corbett Grimes, the Coast's
best story-teller and her sister
Alvina married Al Gear of
Little Sur.
— Collection of Frank Trotter

and Danis at Lucia raised both cattle and hogs, and it was said
that their hogs had to be very fat to reach the market at King

The old Ed Grimes ranch house near the top of the ridge on the Coast trail below Big Sur.
It had a beautiful grape arbor.   — Photo by author

City in good enough condition to sell. (The trip took about two days.) It was easier with the cattle, for they could graze along the way.

In 1875, only two years after David Castro moved to Big Sur from Soberanes, Charlie Bixby and John William Gilkey settled at Mill Creek, halfway between Monterey and the Big Sur, along with the Cunningham brothers. Indians moved into the Little Sur to work at the silver and copper mines there. The Partington brothers, with Bert Stevens, a bachelor and short story writer, started a tanbark and lumber mill at Partington Canyon and they made a tunnel in the rock, which it took three years to build,

PARTINGTON CANYON

Partington Cove where tanbark, pickets, railway ties and lumber were shipped out during the 1890s. Other landings were at Anderson Creek, Bixby Landing and Nottley's Landing at the Palo Colorado.   — Collection of author

and a boat landing at Partington Cove. (The tunnel still exists, along with the ruined boat landing.) The Anderson brothers also had a landing at Anderson Creek, and, like the Partingtons, shipped out tan oak, railway ties, fence posts, lumber, board and shakes. Other boat landings sprang up at Nottley's (at the mouth of Palo Colorado Canyon) and Bixby Landing at Mill Creek (Bixby Creek). For here, too, there were lumber and tanbark mills. It was during this period that the much beloved woodsman, Sam Trotter, settled on the Coast working with the Nottley brothers, Al and Ed. In addition there were two limekilns, one at Mill Creek (Bixby) and the other at Limekiln Creek south of Big Sur near Lucia. The Los Burros gold mine was the most profitable of these ventures, but by the turn of the century it too had shut down. Several Indian families lived at Lucia in the 1870s and took up homesteads, but they got cheated out of their lands; it is said it was because they didn't speak English and didn't realize the import of the papers they were signing. Eventually this part of the Coast became know as the Harlan and Dani strongholds. Miss Lulu May Harlan,

Wilber Judson and Ada Amanda (Dani) Harlan. Married July 7, 1889 in Santa Cruz, California.   —Collection of Irene Harlan

who never married and died in 1984 at the age of 93, for years ran a tourist resort at Lucia while still making her home on the old family homestead, built in the 1870s, atop the mountain.

Homestead cabin of Wilber Judson Harlan. Built in 1885 of split redwood logs. Fireplace of brick, brought to site by mule pack. Lucia—South of Big Sur.
—Collection of Irene Harlan

It was told on the Coast that all the school teachers who came to Lucia ended up marrying one of the Harlan boys and were forever having to be replaced.

* * *

Gabriel and Elizabeth (Brown) Dani married in the spring of 1863 on the Oregon Trail. They were homesteaders, and raised ten children near Lucia on the Big Sur South Coast 1876-1907.
—Collection of Irene Harlan

When the Posts returned to Big Sur after eleven years in Castroville, they found the scene unbelievably changed. They had left a solitary and somber landscape, uninhabited except for the vaqueros at *El Sur*, the hermit Davis, and the whalers at Point Lobos. Now in almost every canyon, from Carmel to Lucia and beyond, the ring of the axe was heard. And Charlie Bixby, who had arrived two years earlier in 1875 had built a wagon road from Point Lobos (part of the Alexander M. Allen ranch) to his place at Mill Creek — a tremendous feat. Later Bixby extended it farther south to the top of Serra Hill, overlooking Little Sur. This was to enable him to haul timber from his ranch at Bixby Mountain. He also built a wagon road down through the canyon to Bixby Landing in order to ship out loads of lumber and tanbark which were lowered via cable to the waiting holds of ships anchored below. It was a tricky operation and it took experts to do it successfully. Later on, the Monterey Lime Company put in an aerial tramway on top of Longridge Mountain from the limekiln three miles up the canyon to Bixby Landing in order to ship out barrels of lime. It is said that many a romance started when the aerial tramway broke down, and that one time a couple, who had never met before, was stranded there all night. A few days later they got married.

Wilber and Ada Harlan's two story home that Wilber built from local redwood that he sawed by waterpower on a Muhly sawmill. It was built about 1900 and burned to the ground in 1926 from chimney sparks.   — Collection of Irene Harlan

Post bought most of his lumber from Bixby to build his ranch house but the rest he split on his own land with the help of his two stalwart, able-bodied sons, Frank and Joe, now respectively 17 and 14 years old. The boards he made were twelve inches across and half an inch thick. He used a draw knife to dress them and he made his own window frames and doors.

One time, when Post and his oldest son, Frank, were away on a trip in the mountains hunting deer, Joe Post was there with his mother and his two sisters when a desperate neighbor from the south rode up on horseback asking for help. His five year old daughter was ill; he needed a doctor; he had to get back to her as she was there alone. In those days the nearest doctor was at Castroville, a very long trip from Big Sur. Without a word being said, Mrs. Post saddled up a horse and packed a bag of food for the 14 year old Joe Post and he left the ranch at a gallop. He changed horses in Monterey, then went on to Castroville where he found the doctor and persuaded him to go back with him. Joe Post conducted the doctor down to the ranch where the sick child was, then collapsed at home, exhausted. The little girl lived. When questioned years later, about this heroic episode Joe Post said, "Oh it was nothing much, just something one did for a neighbor. But I will say I was tired the next day. Anyway I went out to help Dad and Frank with the timber."

The Posts' closest neighbors to the south were David Castro and his alcoholic father, Cristobal. Father and son had come originally from Ensenada, Mexico, during the Gold Rush, and young Castro, as a lad of fourteen, worked for Miller and Lux, carrying payrolls to protect them from bandits. Later he ended up at *El Sur* as a vaquero. It was said that he was the best roper in all of California.

"If a bird would fly low enough, I could catch it," he was wont to remark.

Lizzie Post (Elizabeth Gilkey Post), wife of Joe Post, with her son Joseph W. Post) later known as Willy. Her father was John Gilkey; her father-in-law was W.B. Post, the pioneer.   — Collection of William Post III

In the 1880s a feud sprang up between Post and Castro. No one knew what it was about, but Castro was so angry that he was determined to kill Post. For this purpose he planted a potato patch on his ranch close to the trail, waiting for Post to come riding by.

"One day Post came along riding behind his daughter," Dr. Jaime de Angulo, the noted ethnologist, told me years later.

"And Castro lifted a shovel to hit him. But Post spurred his horse and caught up with his daughter."

Post continued riding down the trail but he was always accompanied by his daughter. Months went by; Castro waited; the potatoes were ready to be dug up from the ground; but he could never find the man alone. Finally he gave up in disgust.

"I can never get that coward." he declared.

In 1870, David Castro had met and married Amadia Vasquez. She was first cousin to the notorious bandit, Tiburcio Vasquez, the so-called Robin Hood of California. Everyone, except those he robbed, regarded him as a hero. Whenever Tiburcio needed to hole up, he and his men headed for the Big Sur and hid out near Lucia, beyond the Castro place. David Castro's eight children grew up with their bandit cousin as a role model. None became bandits, however. Rojelio, the oldest, was called Roche— also *Chanate* or Blackbird because of his shining black hair and was much influenced by Tiburcio but more by his personality than by his actions. He did make bootleg whiskey during Prohibition days, but he never stole. One day the Revenue men came down to Big Sur, and the gracious Amadia, who spoke no English but knew the rules of Spanish etiquette, offered the men refreshments.
"It's right up there, behind the trees," she told them. Thus they were led to Roche's still. But Roche was let off on probation. His real claim to fame was that he bit another man's ear off in a jealous rage at a dance at Nottley's Landing. Robinson Jeffers referred to this in *Californians.*

As the country filled up in the 1870s, 1880s, and 1890s, it began to become a loose-knit community in which there were close ties between neighbors even though they seldom saw each other. They had to depend on each other in case of emergency. There were also many inter-marriages between

Down Coast families. Visiting could be done only in the winter time when there was no outdoor work or else on special occasions such as annual round-ups at *El Sur*, at the Cooper ranch in Little Sur, and the apple harvesting bee at the Post ranch. After filling the barrels with apples at the harvest, neighbors got together, gossiped and exchanged recipes. This was also an occasion for the courting of young people.

Living conditions were primitive due to isolation. Many women living at Big Sur and beyond did all their cooking on fireplaces and used tallow candles, but soon wood stoves, hauled on horseback from Monterey, and kerosene lamps began to make their appearance. No one had running water. Water had to be hauled in buckets from a nearby creek or spring and the out-house was universal. Big sur residents began to feel the need for a road.

"The wagon road went as far as Mill Creek when we moved down to Big Sur," Frank Post elaborated, "Fussell owned in Mill Creek and Little Sur. We ordered supplies from San Francisco. We bought only smaller items in Monterey. One

Old Dani Barn at Pico Blanco.   —Collection of author

or two neighbors would go up and do the buying in San Francisco. The stuff came down by steamer and the boat landed at the mouth of Big Sur River. Then the settlers packed it the rest of the way. We'd order 100 pounds of flour etc., at a time—stuff for the winter."

Down at Lucia, the Harlans and Danis raised wheat and ground it into flour and dried sea water in order to extract the salt.

These supply ships came only once a year, and landed, after the stop at Big Sur, at Big Creek where Lucia residents and their neighbors for miles around both north and south rushed to the Landing when they heard the boat whistle. There was no real landing at Big Creek, however. Boat load after boat load turned over in the surf.

But despite the boat loads, there were still many items Big Sur residents had to get in Monterey. Since the wagon road ended at Mill Creek, the trip from Mill Creek to Big Sur was by trail and had to be done on horseback. Sping-wagons could not be used. That was how the Post's wood stove reached them—packed on horseback over the rough trail.

"We stored our supplies this side of Carmel River, at Joe Gregg's place, the present site of the artichoke fields," Post related. "We took nine or ten horses and the trip required two days. Escolle ran a store in Monterey and we bought things there. But people on the Coast were stuck all winter on account of high water and slides. Dad wanted a road to his place," Post continued. "J.B.H. Cooper, W.A. Pool of San Miguel Canyon, and, if I'm not mistaken, Monroe of Blanco—old-timers— nearly fell over backwards. They were on the County Board of Supervisors at the time. 'We haven't got any money. You are a fool. You are crazy.' That's the reception Dad got before the Salinas Board of Supervisors. But Dad was determined and we built the road to Dad's place out of our own pockets."

In point of fact, the Supervisors finally granted $200 to build a road, but the $200 was soon used up.

"Many tons of dirt were lifted by pick and shovel," Post said. "The settlers built the road out of their own pockets. Then the County took over and we had to pay taxes on it."

Frank and Joe Post worked six months helping to build the road. Gschwend of Little Sur graded it with a homemade level. Now the Big Sur folk could go all the way to town by spring-wagon and they no longer had to order supplies from San Francisco. The wagon road, completed in 1881, only four years after W.B. Post had returned to the Sur, ended at Post's ranch and made 24 stream crossings in Big Sur River alone. Narrow and winding, it went in and out of every canyon between Carmel and Post's. The trip to town, which settlers usually made only once a year by spring-wagon, took three days. They stopped overnight at Nottley's Landing on their way to town and again on their return staying at Ma Swetnam's boarding house at the mouth of Palo Colorado. (Her husband, I.N. Swetnam, had built the place during the tanbark and lumber era of the 1890s.)

Years later, Professor Benjamin Kurtz, head of the poetry department at U.C. Berkeley, told me that as a young man he spent many a summer at Ma Swetnam's place—mainly to watch Ma Swetnam eat. Her bosom was so large that she had to throw the food into her mouth. Her arms would not reach up over it. She never missed. It was especially fascinating, Dr. Kurtz said, to watch her eat peas. Not a single one landed on the table.

In 1889 the Lighthouse was built at Point Sur. It was sorely needed because the Coast here was fog-bound and hazardous and had been the scene of a major shipwreck. The S.S. *Ventura* had gone down here on April 20, 1873 with the loss of many lives. It was Post and his two strong sons who built

Original Bixby Ranch house, later occupied by the Hogue family. Flavia standing in doorway.   — Collection of author

the road up to the Lighthouse.

From the moment the foghorn started blowing and the light shining through the fog, the sea became safe along this treacherous Coast with its many rocks and strong undercurrents. The foghorn, which had been intended for a lighthouse on the Coast of France, landed at Point Sur accidentally, and the story is told that at the time its deep, resonating tone first rang out, a man named Terry Brandon was out in the mountains looking for his lost bull. When he heard the foghorn, he thought it was his bull bellowing and was infuriated to discover, after the fog cleared, that it was not. Forever afterwards the foghorn was referred to as "Terry Brandon's bull."

Another story has it that an old man named Choppy Casuse thought the foghorn was no good. The light was no good either. "Good light—but she no work." he told people. "Go all the time sad Boo-Boo—but the fog, she creep in all the same."

One of the advantages of the wagon-road was that it brought the U.S. mail.

"The neighbors brought the mail in early days," Frank Post said. "We aked for a regular mail route but the government wouldn't give it to us unless someone would carry the mail free for one year. Then contracts would be given. Kasler did it. We fed him and his horses free of charge."

The following year, 1882, the first official U.S. post office was established at the Post ranch three miles beyond Big Sur and was called Arborlado. A second post office, the Sur, was established shortly afterwards at Mill Creek. At this time Fussell owned the place, later the Hogues, then my mother became postmistress when the Sharpes bought it in 1919.

The mail came down the road from Monterey by horse-drawn mail-stage, but in the winter, when the road was blocked with slides, it had to be packed on horseback. The first motor drawn mail-stage appeared in 1923.

South of Post's there was no wagon road. The Posts extended the trail to Torre Creek, when daughter Mary married José de la Torre and to Grimes Point when Ellen married Ed Grimes who came from Liverpool. Settlers in the region south of Big Sur remained isolated and, on account of this, there was a distinct separation between the Big Sur folk and their neighbors farther south despite blood ties. The distance on horseback was too far for easy visiting. However, when there were dances, rodeos, roundups and barbecues, people gathered from miles around—even from Big Creek and Lucia. But the trip was long and hard, especially for the women and children. This situation continued until the 1920s when the highway was built as far as Anderson Creek. (The old road continued to exist, however; the highway section did not start until after Post's.) Work on the highway was halted, and did not recommence until 1929, the year of the Wall Street Crash.

Then, in 1937, the highway opened all the way between Carmel and San Luis Obispo and everything changed. There were women living on the south Coast who had never been to town in their entire lives. One of them, Miss Lulu May Harlan whom I first met at her old ranch house in 1946, welcomed the highway and progress. She loved the modern improvements that replaced the outhouse and the wood stove and the kerosene lamp. But when she made her first trip out of the country she went to Los Angeles, which she disliked, and quickly returned to her native hills, never to leave again until shortly before her death in 1985.

Sitting on the porch of the original Harlan ranch house up on the mountain that day above Lucia Lodge, Miss Harlan smiled and made a gesture with her out-spread hands.

"The hot pavement made my feet hurt," she told me, "so I took off my shoes and lit out for home."

The sun was shining over the sea below and, in the waves, one could see sea otters floating in the kelp beds. It was easy to understand why Miss Lulu May had come home.

Mill Creek (Bixby Creek) Bridge in 1930 under construction with convict labor. Author walked across it when it was a catwalk between the two pilings at the age of 11. Once started, she had no choice.   — Courtesy of Pat Hathaway

IV.

The Strains of the Varsoviana and the Violin

"I still see him riding old Betty Horse up the Coast Road, with his golden auburn hair flowing, and I hear him saying, "This is a free life, not crowded...'"

F ollowing the death of Captain Cooper in 1871, *El Sur Rancho* was divided between his son, John B.H. Cooper II, his daughter who had married a Spanish civil engineer named Eusebio Molera and another daughter, Mrs. Waller. John Cooper II, in particular, felt an obligation to adhere to the old traditions, so he continued with the spring roundups and rodeos which were often attended by hundreds of people. Vaqueros came down the Coast from Monterey to participate in these gala affairs which lasted three days at a time.

"We had a dance hall by the river," John Cooper III, the grandson of the old sea captain told me, "and people danced country dances—the quadrille, the *varsoviana*. One night Tom Oliver, the undertaker from Monterey who later married into the Gregg family, appeared at the dance. He was dressed neatly and well. He was wearing a red shirt, a necktie and a new suit. The other men had overalls. All the girls danced with Tom Oliver. The other men tried to figure out how to spoil his suit. He wanted to get some water for his coffee. One of the men said, "That door, there. . .' There was a deep hole in the river just outside the door. He walked into the hole. So he had to change into overalls. But he still got dances. Finally, when the men said, 'He's a nice man, but he's just out of San Quentin,' the girls stopped dancing with him. Father denied this story. He said it never happened."

During these annual three day affairs of dancing and barbequeing and watching the vaqueros rope and castrate the steers, the women slept in the house, the men in haystacks.

"There were whole beeves hanging under the trees," John Cooper III related, "and we had milk pans full of cooked meat. Women brought cakes and pies. They used honey instead of sugar. For music we had the accordian and guitar. There was plenty of water and lemonade at dances. The lemonade came as a yellow powder in a paper can made by the Smith

Company, already prepared. We also had coffee and tea."

No liquor was served. But those who wanted to drink brought their own and hid it outside in the trees or haystacks. This custom, as recently as the 1950s, was still observed at country dances in the Big Sur. (The women never drank alcohol, however.)

Although Cooper's hospitality flowed lavishly at the annual dances and barbecues, John Cooper II was distressed to find himself trespassed upon by hordes of poor settlers who had moved into Little Sur Canyon in the 1880s and 1890s. Originally most of them had worked in the silver and copper mines along with the Indians, but when these ventures failed they had no way to make a living.

"Our cattle disappeared," Cooper told me. "We gave them meat. Father said, 'Offer 50 cents and help yourself.' For 50 cents they would take a quarter of a steer or 50 pounds. The settlers also got beans from the ranch. All they had to buy was flour, coffee and honey in town."

Another problem was bandits.

"Father used to put a sack of money on the dresser for travellers. He never counted it before or after they came. There were bandits around and Father was afraid of bandits."

"My grandmother never came to the ranch," Cooper went on, "not even when the wagon road went through. She lived to be nearly one hundred. She didn't trust banks. She didn't understand them. She would give a check for $1,000 but not a $5 gold piece."

The old lady died in 1913 at the age of 99. Doña Encarnacion de Vallejo Cooper had been born in 1814, the daughter of one of the most powerful families in the Spanish province, and she had lived through several important chapters of California history. She had seen it pass from Spanish to Mexican rule, and then, after the arrival of General Fremont in 1846, to American rule. She had seen the rise and fall of the sea otter industry under her husband's leadership, and she had survived, with him, the reversal of their fortunes due to American squatters during the Gold Rush. She had watched Monterey turn into a ghost town in the 1850s, and then, after the turn of the century, begin to build up again as a center of the

Doña Encarnacion de Vallejo Cooper, wife of Captain J.B.R. Cooper. The daughter of Ignacio de Vallejo, her brother was General Mariano Vallejo and her nephew was Governor Juan B. Alvarado.
— Collection of Amelie Elkinton

fishing industry with the arrival of Peter Ferrante and the Sicilians. When Doña Encarnacion died so did an era, a tradition—a world.

Her descendants carried on the Spanish way of life, but in 1928 Martha Cooper Hughes, the widow of John Cooper II, sold the Little Sur part of the ranch to Harry Hunt of Pebble Beach, thus bringing to a close forever the era of great rodeos and dances and the strumming of guitars.

Others went on, however with the Cooper tradition as well as they could, and neighbors got together for spring roundups at various cattle ranches in the Sur unitl the 1950s. The dance hall at Nottley's Landing, which came into existence during the turbulent tanbark era, to some extent took the place of the dance hall at *El Sur*, but it never had the same elegance or romance. Indeed, the Saturday night gatherings at Nottley's were often raucous and even violent affairs. This was a lawless era—in the 1880, '90s and early 1900s—and there were knife fights, murders, even lynchings. During this period the Coast became notorious. In addition to the dance hall at Nottley's, there was a bar at Mill Creek run by West Smith which was frequented by the limekiln workers, mainly Italians, and every Sunday morning dead Italians would be found in the woods. One day, West Smith told me years later, Horace Hogue, who lived across the creek in the old Gilkey ranch house, strolled over to the bar for a chat. He was dressed well, in a suit and necktie, and was wearing a hat. Hogue had originally intended to be a clergyman but had contracted tuberculosis so had come down to visit his uncles at Mill Creek. He married the school teacher, Florence Young, and stayed on. A few minutes after Hogue arrived, a couple of toughs dropped in.

"Let's see the gentleman dance," they cried, and began peppering the floor with gunshots just near his feet, first one and then the other. Poor Horace Hogue was forced to dance to the peppering of gunshots which could not have been very good for his tuberculosis. All the time Sing Fat, the imperturbable Chinaman, who went down the Coast to gather seaweed in his little spring wagon, was sitting at the bar. He

Horace Hogue, the would-be clergyman who came down with tuberculosis. He went to Mill Creek to visit his uncles, fell in love with the local school teacher and married her. Here he remained until his death.
— Collection of Elizabeth Hogue Van Der Pleough

seemed to be oblivious to the affair. After the toughs departed, West turned to him and said, "Sing Fat, what would you have done if they had turned their guns on you?"

Sing Fat responded with a broad grin and opened his jacket. He was carrying a double-barrelled shotgun and had had it trained on the two men the whole time.

"I'd have taken care of them, don't worry about that," he said in perfect English. He'd never been known to speak English before.

Sing Fat was one of the enigmas of the Coast, and it was not discovered until after his death that he lived in a little cabin in the mountains.

A prominent figure during these times was John William Gilkey, who had settled at Mill Creek in 1875 and built a ranch house there. He then moved away, returned, settled at Rocky Creek, then Big Sur. He ended his days at a hotel in Monterey. It was his daughter, Amy Melissa Gilkey Miller (Mrs. Alfred Miller of Monterey) who told me his story. A native of Missouri, Gilkey was half Cherokee Indian, though he didn't look it for he was auburn-haired and had a long auburn beard which he curled.

"He was quite a dandy," the old timers said.

Gilkey played the violin and was always moving from place to place. He was of Irish and Scotch descent on his father's side, Indian on his mother's. His mother had a place at Prunedale, near the bandit Joaquin Murietta's legendary hideout, where he met Charlie Bixby. This was in 1875 and Bixby was moving down the Coast south of Monterey to the country known as the Sur. Bixby persuaded Gilkey to move down there along with Ed and Kenneth Cunningham. They all acquired land at Mill Creek where Bixby, a resourceful man, raised cattle and hogs in addition to building roads, shipping out lumber and tanbark and operating a boat landing. Gilkey did not stay long, however. Soon after he had built the house he got word that his grandmother was dying back in Missouri. He wanted to see her before she died. So he sold his place to Thomas Fussell, packed up his family in a spring wagon and took off.

"There were five of us children," Mrs. Miller told me. "Myself, Sylvester, Cyrus, Alva and Elizabeth. I went to school with Alta Gregg who used to be Alta Bixby—Charlie Bixby's daughter. My father played for Coast dances. When we lived at Rocky Creek, after we left Mill Creek, he used to walk all the way from Rocky Creek to Little River for dances. His violin had come across the plains three times."

It was in the fall of the year when the Gilkeys left Mill Creek for Missouri, so they took the southern route. When they got to Albuquerque they had to stop because of an Indian outbreak. Many people had been killed and the Gilkeys slept in a house where an entire family had just been buried. Finally they decided it was safe to go on, but this proved to be false.

"On the way from Albuquerque, Indians saw Pop with the wagon," Amy Gilkey Miller recounted. "'We're gone,' he said. Soldiers were just ahead of us but out of sight. Pop had a rifle he called Old Sweet Lips. 'I'll fight 'em off as long as I can,' he said. He piled bedding on us children so we would not be hit by arrows. 'Give me my violin,' he said. He put down the rifle. He played the violin. Pop had beautiful auburn hair. He was playing for dear life. The Indians stopped. They listened. Pop played loud. Finally they bowed on their horses and off they went. He played loud but it was soft music. It was more music of the soul than anything I have ever heard."

Mrs. Miller stopped, tears in her eyes. "Pop's music saved us," she said.

Five miles later they caught up with the column of soldiers.

"How did you escape?" the Captain asked.

"No fault of yours," said Gilkey. The soldiers had passed them en route, knowing about the Indians, but had given no word of warning.

They returned to Albuquerque where they ran into another Indian outbreak and somehow the family got separated. As soon as the worst of it was over, Mrs. Gilkey borrowed a wagon and horses to take the children back to California, thinking that her husband was dead. John Gilkey remained in New Mexico, hiding out there after still another Indian attack had nearly cost him his life. In the house where he was staying, a grandmother and a little girl were murdered and scalped, and Gilkey barely escaped.

"We didn't see Father for three years," Amy Miller related. "We thought he was dead. We came back to Monterey. Later we found out that after the Indian attack, Father had to hide out. He nearly starved to death. He got ulcers."

John Gilkey never recovered from this terrible experience. He was in ill health the rest of his life on account of it.

In Monterey, Mrs. Gilkey supported her family by running a boarding house. After Gilkey's unexpected return, they moved back down the Coast to Rocky Creek, later to the Big Sur where they had a place in the mountains behind Post's. Amy Gilkey Miller's sister Elizabeth (Lizzie) married Joe Post and it was she who was killed by her horse years later.

John Gilkey died in 1900 at the St. Charles Hotel in Monterey, still suffering from ulcers but with his beloved violin beside hin.

Mrs. Miller's final comment on her father was, "I still see him riding old Betty Horse up the Coast Road, with his golden auburn hair flowing, and I hear him saying, "This is a free life, not crowded...'"

Dr. Roberts' mansion located on the dunes high above Del Monte Beach
—Collection of John L.D. Roberts II.

V.

Coast Doctor

His greatest dream was to see a highway built along the Coast between Carmel and San Luis Obispo. ... He felt that a highway would not only make life easier for the inhabitants of the region, especially for those around Lucia, but would make this scenic landscape accessible to everyone. As it was, no one knew its beauty save those who lived there. It belonged, he felt, to the state, the nation, the world.

T he first doctor to go down to the Sur was Dr. John L.D. Roberts in the year 1887. He had recently arrived in Monterey with one dollar in his pocket and his medical degree. A native of Osceola, New York, he had gotten his medical training at the University of New York and Columbia University, then done a two year internship and practice at the New York Hospital and in the Insane Asylum at Utica, New York. Born in 1861, he was 26 years old. Engaged to a girl named Edith Maltby, he was uncertain as to where he wanted to practice. He had two uncles living in Monterey, California; one of them, Walter Dodge, ran a blacksmith shop the other, D.J. Houghton, had a painting and paper-hanging establishment, and they wrote him that Monterey was the ideal place to set up a practice. A doctor was urgently needed. The only doctor they had in Monterey, they wrote, was "a genuine quack" named J.P. Heinz. Heinz had never been to medical school. And, in addition to illegally practicing medicine, he was the local barber, undertaker, and embalmer.

"You will be doing the community a genuine service," they wrote, "if you come and put Heinz out of business." Heinz's doings, they went on, were indeed a scandal. When the famous Josh Billings died at the elegant Del Monte Hotel, Heinz charged $1,500 for embalming him, then threw the guts under a bridge in Monterey where the dogs ate them. This was the way Heinz habitually disposed of human entrails. Later, John Steinbeck mentioned this in *Tortilla Flat*.

Once in Monterey, where young Roberts arrived on January 5, 1887, he found that things were not as simple as they had sounded at a distance.

"Heinz had the town sewed up," Doc Roberts told me, "It would have been impolitic to go into competition with him."

He was getting ready to return East when someone suggested he might try becoming a country doctor. There was land on

Daisy

Dr. John L.D. Roberts and his horse, Daisy, setting forth in his two-wheel cart to tend to the sick on the Sur Coast. He was in practice there (and in Monterey) for over a decade.
—Courtesy of Monterey Public Library

the Coast south of Carmel where hundreds of people lived without a doctor. He would be welcomed, and was certainly needed. So Doc Roberts went down the old Coast road and introduced himself. Within a week he had been called upon to vaccinate 156 children in the Little Sur, and from then on he was in business. Often in an emergency, even in the middle of the night, Doc Roberts would saddle up his horse and go down to the Sur at a gallop. More usually however, medicine bag in hand, he rode down there in a two wheel cart pulled by his horse, Daisy.

The encouragement of his practice on the Coast and his friendship with the residents there persuaded him to try, after all, the practice of medicine in Monterey regardless of Heinz. So he rented an office near the corner of Polk and Harnell Streets in Monterey and sent for his fiancee and married her on October 25, 1887. The marriage took place at the home of his uncle, E.J. Houghton, on Cass Street, and Miss Maltby's father, J.B.S. Maltby, came out from New York to give her away in marriage. He stayed for six months and liked the place so well that he went back to Troy, New York, sold his business and moved permanently to Monterey with his wife, Sarah.

Young Dr. Roberts fell in love with the beauty of the Sur country, and with its inhabitants whom he came to know well and intimately. He practiced there for 12 years.

"There was only a dirt road, crooked as a ram's horn. If I had a long way to go, I'd change horses on the way, usually at Tom Doud's place." This was at Soberanes Creek, a few miles south of Point Lobos.

The most dramatic call he ever made was when the S.S. Los Angeles was wrecked off Point Sur on April 21, 1894, almost twenty years to the day after the wreck of the S.S. Ventura. The Los Angeles was a small boat with a crew of 36 and 69 passengers but it was also carrying hundreds of head of livestock. Doc Roberts was called about five o'clock in the evening and set off in his two wheel cart, drawn by Daisy. When he got to the Doud Ranch at midnight, he found Tom Doud waiting for him with a lantern. "You can never make it with this horse and cart," he told him. "I'll lend you my stallion."

Doud's stallion was a fiery one, and it took three men to subdue him and hitch him to the cart. Even at a fast pace, it was a rough ride in the darkness over a very bad road. According to legend, the trip from Doud's ranch to Point Sur Lighthouse beach took 3 hours, which would have meant he arrived there around 3 a.m. but Doc Roberts himself told me a different story. He said he got there at dawn and that the sight that met his eyes was horrifying. Many bodies were stacked on the beach and, at first sight, he thought they were all human. As it turned out, most were cattle.

"A strange and gruesome sight," said Roberts, "was the presence of over 100 calves among the humans. They were all drowned and their legs stuck up out of the water and sand."

Doc Roberts, father of Seaside, served on the County Board of Supervisors for 20 years, was Seaside postmaster for 30 years, and was responsible for the building of the Carmel-San Simeon Highway.   — Courtesy of the City of Seaside

Many of the crew and passengers (about a hundred in all) were dead, others dying. All who survived were suffering from shock and exposure. Single-handed, Dr. Roberts administered first aid, working day and night for three days, and saved most of them. He embalmed the dead. The most dramatic part of it, however, was rescuing the captain and first mate, who, true to the tradition of the sea, had stayed with the sinking ship. They lived. Later on, when Doc Roberts put in a bill of $200 for his services, the master of the wrecked vessel refused to pay him. Years later, Doc Roberts collected when the sea captain put into port at Monterey.

In the course of his practice in the Sur, Doc Roberts encountered many dramatic happenings which he took great pleasure in recounting after his retirement.

"Around about sundown," Doc Roberts told me, when he was staying overnight at the Gilkey house in Rocky Creek, "when we were about to sit down for supper, some men came along, greatly excited. 'A man has just been murdered on Serra Hill,' they cried. 'Glad you're here, Doc. Come with us.' The murdered man was Billy Hansen. Billy Hansen had been squatting on Serra Hill on the other side of the Hitchcock place, near Maria Heath and her daughter Serena. Somebody wanted his ranch and he refused to sell. 'The men who wanted the ranch must have shot him,' they said."

Doc Roberts and the auburn-haired John Gilkey accompanied the men up Serra Hill and found that Billy Hansen's corpse had been carried to the Charlie Howland place. They rode over to view the body.

"Billy Hansen had two bullets in his brain," Doc Roberts recalled, "But he wasn't dead. After removing the bullets, I put him on a stretcher and we carried him down to the Gayety place in Little Sur, and I asked Mrs. Gayety to look after him."

Billy Hansen recovered. But the next time Doc Roberts went down the Coast he found that Billy Hansen had disapperared.

"Somebody spirited him away," he was told.

A few weeks later he ran into a man on Serra Hill, riding a mule.

"He was red-haired and his long hair was flying back in the wind and he was naked except for a red shirt and a g-string. He slid to a stop when he saw me and he produced a rope. 'We got the s.o.b. that got Billy Hansen,' he said, 'We're going to have a little necktie party tonight, Doc, want to come along'?"

"I questioned him," Doc Roberts continued, "and found that old man Snow down in the Sur was the unfortunate man blamed. 'Why the poor old man couldn't shot a goose,' I said. But the red-haired man wouldn't listen. I hurried down to the Gayety place and told young Gayety to go down to Big Sur on horseback and warn Snow. 'Get on your mustang and ride to Pfeiffer's,' I told him. Young Gayety went. By the time the mob arrived at Big Sur a few hours later old man Snow was gone. There was no lynching."

Many years later, when Doc Roberts was practicing medicine in Big Oak Flat near Sonora, he ran into Billy Hansen who was there mining gold.

"I questioned him, naturally. He told me that he had sold his ranch for $1,500 to the people who had tried to murder him. And I collected my long over-due medical bill," he dryly added.

A few months after the Billy Hansen episode, Mrs. Gayety's husband became infatuated with a Mrs. Cunningham who lived on the hill near the top of Little Sur grade, and moved in with her, leaving Mrs. Gayety alone at the ranch.

"Mrs. Cunningham was a good-looking old gal," Doc Roberts remarked.

"One day on my way down the Coast I met up with a tramp with a bundle on his back. His name was Frank Halickas. He said he was looking for a job as a hired man. I told him to go to the Gayety place. Maybe Mrs. Gayety needed someone, I said. The next time I went down there I found Halickas had been hired and was sitting down eating breakfast with Mrs. Gayety. The door opened and Gayety walked in. He read his wife the riot act. He was jealous," Doc Roberts remarked.

Mrs. Gayety listened in silence.

"Finally Frank Halickas spoke up. 'He talks kinder big,' he

said. Mrs. Gayety nodded. 'Take him out and throw him in the river,' she said."

Frank Halickas, who was a big man, picked up Gayety with one hand and threw him in Little Sur River.

"The gentleman landed in the pond," said Doc Roberts.

One night Gayety got drunk with a man named Feininger and they went over Little Sur grade in a spring wagon and were killed. That was the end of Gayety. What happened to Mrs. Gayety and Frank Halickas Doc Roberts did not know.

Doc Roberts' most exciting tale was of a murder he witnessed.

There was a mean old rancher who had married an 18 year old girl. He treated her brutally, used foul language. "All of the bad characters thought he was pretty bad," Doc Roberts said.

One day the rancher broke his leg and sent for Doc Roberts. He went to see him several times after he set the leg, but the more he saw him the more he disliked him. One day, on his way down to the ranch, he came upon an exhausted cowboy, crawling on his hands and knees. He had come all the way up the Coast from San Luis Obispo by trail, and he was in need of medical aid as well as of food. Doc Roberts put him on the back of his saddle and tied him so that he wouldn't fall off. He took him to his patient's ranch and told the convalescent rancher that as part of his medical fee he wanted the cowboy to stay there until he was on his feet again. When he returned three weeks later, he found the rancher in fair condition.

"Unfortunately my patient was recovering, but he still couldn't do any ranch work," Doc Roberts related.

The cowboy, on the other hand, had recovered entirely but was faking illness because he wanted to stay on.

"Why don't you get a job here?" the doctor suggested, and soon the matter was settled; the cowboy was hired.

About three weeks later, on his way up to the house for a final check on the broken leg, Doc Roberts heard a great commotion going on inside. The rancher was shouting and swearing at his wife, just as he had done before the cowboy appeared. The doctor waited outside, listening, not wanting to go in until it was over. In a few mintues' time, the rancher's angry voice was interrupted by thuds, bumps and the sound of a chair crashing, then there was complete silence. The door opened and two figures came out—the rancher in front, the cowboy in back. He was grasping the rancher by the back of his neck and by his crotch. He rushed him over the ground and threw him over the cliff. On his way back to the house, the cowboy suddenly noticed Doc Roberts standing there. His expression didn't change.

"Glad to see you Doc," he said. "And I would like to invite you to the wedding. You probably need some coffee. Won't you come in?"

Doc Roberts went in. The young ranch wife asked no questions, made no comments, but poured coffee for all three of them. They sat down. The cowboy said, "Of course you'll be the best man at our wedding won't you?"

"Yes, I'd like to," Doc agreed. And so he was. No one on the Coast asked any questions about this affair. No one had liked the mean rancher, and they were glad he was dead, no matter how.

But there was one murder that troubled Doc Roberts until the end of his days. This was the death of Adelaide Cushing in the Palo Colorado. When I asked him about it, tears came to his eyes.

The Smith ranch at Rocky Creek (house in background). Originally the Jones house where the girl jumped off the cliff. West Smith turned it into a bar called *Westmere* before Pearl Harbor. Photographed from the north so house is in background.
— Courtesy of Vesta Bauman

"It was a terrible thing," he told me, "She was such a young and pretty girl."

It was Sadie Starrett who first told me about the affair, as she had grown up in the Palo Colorado not far from the Cushing ranch house. Mrs. Cushing, the widow of a sea captain, was a vain, arrogant woman, bad tempered, unkind to her neighbors, and always kept a pistol at her belt. Her daughter, Adelaide, who looked even younger than she actually was, was an artist and very much down-trodden by her domineering mother. She fell in love with a young man named Ned Murray who lived farther up the canyon, and she used to sneak out to meet him whenever her mother went to town in the spring wagon. Adelaide was 26, but her mother did not want her to marry and forbade her seeing young men. It was rumored that she was jealous of her lovely young daughter.

"One day the mother returned from town early and found the girl gone," Sadie Starrett told me. "The girl was soon found shot in the back. They laid her out in the log cabin. After that we called the log cabin the Morgue.

"What happened to her mother?" I asked Sadie.

"Why, we ostracized her," she replied. Ostracism was harsh punishment on this lonely Coast.

"What really happened?" I asked Doc Roberts. "Sadie Starrett said she was shot in the back and her mother did it."

Smith family ranch house viewed from wagon-road. The many bedrooms were needed when there were 10 children.   —Collection of Vesta Bauman

"I performed the autopsy at the cabin they call the Morgue," he said. "The girl had been knifed in the back—not shot. She couldn't have knifed herself in the back. It was passed off as suicide but obviously it was murder. Her mother must have followed her up the canyon and caught her with the young man."

The mother was hated by everyone on the Coast, he added. She kept a locked gate and wouldn't let people pass over her land. School children, including Sadie Starrett, had to walk miles out of their way on this account.

"What happened to Mrs. Cushing in the end?" I asked Doc Roberts.

"Why, she got married again and left the Coast," he told me.

Ned Murray left, too. He went to China and was never heard of again.

Murders were not the only peculiar things the young doctor encountered in the course of his practice on the Sur Coast. One night he stopped in at Jones place, later the Smith ranch, at Rocky Creek for dinner.

"Old man Jones was a religious fanatic," Doc Roberts related. "He was continually quoting the Bible. But everyone said he'd sell you rotten eggs and sour apples. His son, Ed Jones, ran the ranch. He had a daughter, a pretty 17-year-old with auburn hair who had been deeply affected by her father's religion. She began to hear voices of God, and she thought the white caps and the sheen of the water with the sun sparkling upon it were angels. That night we were just sitting down to dinner when suddenly the girl sprang up and cried, 'Jesus is calling me and I've got to go now.' She ran out of the house and across the field. We followed her but we got there too late. She had thrown herself over the cliff."

Richard "Dick" Smith and his wife Helena Kellegher Smith on their wedding day in 1878 at Gonzales, California. —Collection of Gene Fitzpatrick

Her body was badly crushed and Doc Roberts helped carry it up from the rocky beach several hundred feet below. There was sea weed in her auburn hair when they laid her out in her coffin.

"Her father said, 'I saw her soul ascending into heaven like a little lamb,'" Doc Roberts told me.

Years later, after Richard Smith (a descendant of the Cornwallis-West family of England) bought the ranch from Jones and they had to dig up the girl's coffin and move her, they found that her auburn hair had grown through the cracks in the casket.

Doc Roberts' final comment was: "The old man had driven his daughter crazy. Maybe it was just as well she died."

Robinson Jeffers had never heard of old man Jones when he wrote *Give Your Heart to the Hawks* and yet the fanatically religious old man Fraser of the tragic narrative could have been modelled on him, and, to carry coincidence further, Fayne Fraser, like the Jones girl, had red hair. The Jones family had been gone for years before Jeffers visited the Coast in 1914. The Smith family, with their ten children, were much in evidence.

Doc Roberts left his practice on the Coast in 1901, having decided to try his hand at gold mining. He went up to the Mother Lode country near Sonora where he settled at

Richard Smith who bought the old Jones place. A descendant of the aristicratic Cornwallis-West family in England., he named his oldest son West, in honor of it.
—Collection of Vesta Bauman

Helena Smith—the valiant pioneer mother of ten children. She was of Irish descent.
—Collection of Vesta Bauman

Groveland on Big Oak Flat. Here he continued to practice medicine but also to hunt for gold. He struck it rich. He found the famous Longfellow mine, and returned to the Monterey Peninsula with new plans in mind.

In 1887, soon after establishing his practice on the Coast and then in Monterey, he bought a 160 acre piece of land called The Farm from his uncle, D.J. Houghton, in East Monterey. It was his dream to subdivide it and establish a city. The climate there, he told his uncle, was much better than in foggy Pacific Grove. Finally his uncle consented to sell it to him for $5,000, and in six months he had paid for it, plus putting $4,000 in the bank. He owned his own home, and he still had 1,000 more lots to sell. Thus he established the City of Seaside on October 10, 1890.

Before taking off for the gold fields, he founded the Seaside post office and was postmaster there for 32 years.

In 1908, after his return from Groveland, he was elected to the Monterey County Board of Supervisors on which he served as chairman for four years. Altogether he spent 20 years on the Board of Supervisors. He also served on The Board of Trustees for the school district.

His greatest dream was to see a highway built along the Coast between Carmel and San Luis Obispo. As a young doctor, he made the trip on foot from San Luis Obispo to Monterey, the same journey made by the exhausted cowboy he had found crawling on his hands and knees. Halfway along the trail, near the Los Burros Gold Mine, Doc Roberts had collapsed from exhaustion and swollen feet, and had to remain two days in a miner's cabin before he was able to go on again. He had never forgotten this trip along the precipituous Santa Lucias nor the spectacular beauty of the Coastline. He felt that a highway would not only make life easier for the inhabitants of the region, especially for those around Lucia, but would make this scenic landscape accessible to everyone. As it was, no one knew its beauty save those who lived there. It belonged, he felt, to the state, the nation, the world.

in 1915, he convinced Senator Rigdon, of Cambria, of the feasibility of such a highway and spent twenty years of lobbying in Sacramento, with the help of Senator Rigdon, to bring it to pass. At first the proposal was called crazy, impractical and a waste of the taxpayer's money—much the same reception W.B. Post had received from the Monterey County Board of Supervisors in 1881 when he proposed building a wagon road to his ranch below Big Sur. But finally, during the Richardson administration, funds were appropriated and construction began. The road was extended from Post's ranch to Slate's Springs (now called Esalen and formerly Hot Springs Creek) before the funds ran out. The project was halted until around 1930 when the Legislature agreed to complete the highway with convict labor (Doc Roberts had arranged this with a friend who was a prison warden), and it was finally opened to tourist traffic on July 3, 1937, with Doc Roberts as guest of honor at the dedication ceremony held at Bixby Creek Bridge. It was he who cut the ribbon, allowing the first stream of traffic to go through.

Dr. Roberts was proud of the highway, which had been the outstanding achievement of his lifetime, yet he was, at the same time, inevitably nostalgic for the days when there was nothing but the wagon road and he was a young country doctor in a two wheel cart.

Ironically, the highway which brought life to the precipitous sea edge of the Coast and made the world familiar with its spectacular mountains, ended the inland life—the life that had once been its mainstay. And gradually, as the years wore on, especially after the end of World War II, the canyons were all but deserted.

Old Al Clarke, the hermit of Little Sur, who posed as an illiterate but held a Ph.D. from Columbia. People believed he had found the secret of the lost Indian gold, but said that he returned "in the guise of a madman."   —Courtesy of Ruby Gear Woicekowski

VI.

More on Doc Roberts: The Legend of Leather Britches & the Mystery of Old Man Clarke

Al Clarke claimed it was wrong to use gold the way people use it. Gold was what was wrong with civilization. Since he had found the secret, he told Doc Roberts, he did not need to use it. If he used it, he lost it. In other words, the true value of the gold was its concept or essence, what might be termed its spiritual value. It possessed magical powers, such as crystals do. It had been misused for material purposes and mankind was paying the consequences of this.

T he last time I saw Doc Roberts was out at his house on the sand dunes overlooking Del Monte Beach and Monterey Bay. In 1946, it was the only house in sight, and it was a huge, concrete, gray square structure. The view was breathtaking; the wind endless. Doc Roberts' beloved wife Edith was dead; he was losing his eyesight and was nearly stone deaf. I had to communicate with him by putting my mouth close to his one "good ear" and shouting into it. He was 85.

"Florence Hogue, the school teacher, tells me you used to be a very handsome young man," I screamed. "She said all the ladies down the Coast were crazy about you and used to wait for you to ride by. You caused lots of heart throbs. Did you know that?"

"Humph," said Doc Roberts. "Handsome is as handsome does."

He was enraged that day because the Department of Motor Vehicles had refused to renew his driver's license on the grounds that he couldn't see and couldn't hear.

"Can you imagine that?" he stormed. "I've driven a car all these years and they never asked me to take a test before. Maybe I can't see and I can't hear but I can still drive."

"It's a darned shame," I shouted piercingly.

"I'll tell you what I'm going to do," he went on, "and I wish you'd put it on the front page of the newspaper. I'm going to get out the old horse and buggy and I'm going to get me a couple of horses. There's no law against driving a horse and buggy without a license."

"What a wonderful idea," I screamed.

"I'll drive right down Alvarado Street," he said, "and stop traffic."

Alvarado was the main street in Monterey.

It would indeed have caused a sensation if the eminent Doc Roberts had carried through with his idea, but fortunately or unfortunately as the case may be, his son, Houghton, put a stop to it.

A story he never tired of telling, and which he repeated to me this day, was of the time he was gold mining at Big Oak Flat. He and his wife, Edith, were living in a little lean-to outside Groveland and a man suddenly walked in with a gun in his hand.

"Come with me," the stranger ordered.

"Where to?" asked Doc Roberts.

The man wouldn't answer. "Come," he said, pointing his gun at him.

Doc Roberts went, leaving his wife Edith worried to put it mildly.

Outside the man blindfolded him and put him on a horse. Then he led him to a cabin up in the hills where he had a coffin and a dead body. The dead body wouldn't fit the coffin. He had made the coffin before killing the man and hadn't measured him.

"Make him fit," he ordered the doctor.

So Doc Roberts got out his surgical implements and cut the man's legs off at the knees. Now he could be fitted into the too-short coffin. He helped with the burial; then his blindfold was put back on and he was conducted back to the little lean-to where Mrs. Roberts was frantically awaiting him, not knowing whether she would ever see him again.

"Thanks, Doc," said the mysterious stranger and disappeared into the night.

Doc Roberts never found out who the man was, who had been murdered or where he had been that night.

"Did you know Leather Britches?" I asked Doc that day.

Doc Roberts laughed a little ruefully.

"Well, she was a big stalwart woman with a big red face like a pumpkin," he told me. "And she had a daughter, Serena, who was as big and strong as she was. I stayed overnight at their house on Serra Hill one time, but I never did it again because my bed was full of bugs."

"How about the murder?" I screamed into his ear. "Did she really kill that hired man? And was she a cattle rustler?"

"Humph," said Doc Roberts, sounding rather like a camel, "I don't think I'll talk about that. Maria Heath was all right. She wasn't as bad as people said she was."

In any case, I had already heard plenty of lurid versions of the tale of Leather Britches.

Originally she had settled on part of the *San Jose y Sur Chiquito* grant near the Doud ranch at Soberanes Creek, but she made herself unpopular with her neighbors because, as they put it, "all of her cows had twin calves." If she had been a man, they would have lynched her. As it was they left the lady alone.

Eventually she moved farther south to Serra Hill, later the Brazil ranch, not far above our place at Mill Creek.

There are numerous versions as to how she came to be called Leather Britches, or *Calsanutha* as it was in Spanish. According to one story, John Gilkey had a handsome pair of leather britches and one day they disappeared. He couldn't find them anywhere. On his way to town a few months later he met Mrs. Heath who was riding astride her horse and he noticed that under her riding skirt she was wearing his leather britches.

He said, "Mrs. Heath, give me $10 or I'll take those pants right off you."

She took them off and gave them back to him.

Another version has it that she stole them from a hired man.

One afternoon she and the hired man were up in the pasture, and as Mrs. Heath vaulted over the corral fence he saw, under her skirt, his leather britches.

Whatever story is true (and there are still other versions) the fact remains that Maria Heath stole someone's leather britches and was nicknamed, on this account, *Calsanutha*.

But the thing for which Mrs. Heath was chiefly notorious was that she shot and killed, either accidentally or otherwise, one of her hired men—possibly the one from whom she stole the famous leather britches. Some of the old-timers claim that after his death she was seen wearing them again.

The story I was told at the age of three was a blood curdling one. One day I was standing on the front porch of our ranch house at Rainbow Lodge and my grandfather, the retired Colonel, was with me. I pointed to the blackened trestles of the old limekiln aerial tramway on Longbridge Mountain, and my grandfather said sternly, "Little ladies don't point." A neighbor was with us. "Oh, the child is pointing at more than she thinks she is," he said, and went on to tell us that there was a graveyard up there, just behind the fire-blackened trestles, where markers were laid out in neat rows, all painted white. This was where, over the years, Mrs. Heath had buried her hired men, one by one, every time they asked for their wages. She had carried the bodies clear from her ranch on Serra Hill up to Lodgridge on horseback. (An improbable tale, I may add.) Every time a man went to work for her she shot him the moment he asked for his overdue wages.

People were so frightened of Mrs. Heath on account of this and other equally gruesome, widely circulated tales that when they got down into Mill Creek and up Serra Hill they spurred their horses to a gallop and prayed. Everyone was afraid of her except for an Indian boy from Big Sur who had never even heard of her. One day he met her on the road and said politely, "Buenas días, Senora." She was so startled at being spoken to in kindly accents that she turned and fled, as though the very devil were at her heels.

According to Harvey Abbott, who was born on Serra Hill near the Heath property, Mrs. Heath had shot only one hired man—and she did indeed shoot him, but Harvey thought it was probably accidental. (He was not certain, however.) Everytime the man asked Mrs. Heath for his wages, she put him off. Finally he got tired of this. He issued an ultimatum. Either he would get his pay next day or he would leave the ranch. She put him off as usual. So he said he was definitely leaving next day and expected the full amount of his overdue wages. This time Mrs. Heath agreed. He rode around the neighborhood to say goodbye to all his friends. He stopped in at Richard Smith's ranch, the Harvey Abbott place, and the Hitchcocks, to tell them of his forthcoming departure.

But to their surprise, he didn't come riding out the next day or the day after that. They kept watching for his horse but it didn't turn up. They began to wonder what had happened. A day or two later, Mrs. Heath appeared on the road with a body tied on the back of her saddle. She explained that there had been an accident in which he had gotten shot. She was taking his body to town to report the incident to the Sheriff's office.

A neighbor advised her, "No, Mrs. Heath, you'd better not do that. You'd better just take him home and bury him."

So she started back to the ranch. When nearly there, someone else told her, "You'd better take the body into town. Otherwise people will think you murdered him." So she started back to town. Along the road she met someone else who said, "Let sleeping dogs lie."

Thoroughly confused, Maria Heath wandered back and forth along the wagon road until "the body rotted off the saddle."

Improbable as this may seem, a real "tall tale," there can be little doubt that this was indeed the case. Harvey Abbott himself told me he saw the partially decomposed body, smelling to high heaven, as she rode back and forth along the wagon road, seeming not to know what to do with it.

West Smith of Rocky Creek, the same one who had once had a bar at Mill Creek, had an even gorier version—but then West was a real teller of tall tales. (He, like my mother, "elaborated".) He told bar customers at Westmere, his bar in the old Smith ranch house, that Mrs. Heath rode up and down the Coast with the man's body on the back of her saddle, boasting of the fact that she had killed him; and that everyone, in terror, got out their best silverware and china and entertained her royally for fear the same fate might happen to them.

Lynda Sargent of the *Carmel Cymbal*, a weekly newspaper, had yet another version, in which it was Serena Heath who had been shot to death by her mother.

Doc Roberts sneered at this.

"Serena moved to Berkeley after her mother died," he said. "They sold out to Antone Brazil, who came from the Azores Islands, and Jack and Tony Brazil, his sons, married two of the Dani girls. Katherine and Margaret. But I expect you know about that."

"Yes," I said.

"Things were much quieter on Serra Hill after the Heaths moved out. I'll say that," Doc Roberts added.

"How about old man Clarke?" I asked. "Your grandson says you were a great friend of his."

Dr. Roberts paused and appeared to ponder.

"Old man Clarke was very psychic," he told me. "Everytime I went down to the Little Sur, he used to meet me on the road. Sometimes he'd be late and come rushing down the canyon. 'I knew you were coming, Doc,' he'd cry. Sometimes I'd hear him half a mile away. 'I'll be right there.'"

Doc Roberts paused.

"It's all right to talk about Al Clarke now, for he's dead."

Al Clarke had died in Monterey at the age of 94 in 1936. He left the Little Sur only a few months earlier, too old and feeble to continue living alone as a hermit. John Roberts II and I had often come upon his rusty camp stoves at various spots in the south fork of the Little Sur, one of them near Al Gear's place at the foot of Pico Blanco. Al Gear, who was the only other regular inhabitant of the Little Sur, had married Alvina Dani, the daughter of Alvin Dani. And her sister, Electa, had married Corbett Grimes and lived at the old Swetnam house at the Palo Colorado. (They had bought it from Sam Trotter.) Her father Alvin Dani, said of Electa that she was the best cattlewoman on the entire coast and better than any man. Al Gear packed all his supplies three miles up the south fork of Little Sur River on foot, then up a steep trail.

Al Clarke built himself a cabin but stayed there only part of the time. He was a wanderer. He went from camp site to camp site throughout the canyon and his rusty camp stoves, to this day, can be found there under the shelter of giant redwoods.

Doc Roberts paused in this story. "Yes," I screamed encouragingly.

I waited. Although I had known Al Clarke as a child—he often dropped by our place in his little spring wagon on his way to town or else merely to pay us a visit—I knew from hints young John Roberts had dropped that there was some great mystery connected to him.

"Well," said Dr. Roberts at last. "I promised never to tell anyone but Al Clarke was a fellow student of mine at Columbia."

He paused, registering my shock.

"But he seemed illiterate," I screamed into his ear.

"Yes," he said, "but that was only an act he put on."

Hastily I reviewed my picture of old man Clarke. I had seen him from the earliest time I could remember (probably I was one or two) riding down Serra Hill in his little spring wagon, his beard waving in the breeze, stopping in at our place for a chat. Everybody thought he was crazy. There were other hermits living in the hills, but none like Al Clarke.

Al Clarke talked about gold, the male and female elements of metals, and of marriages between them, and of hearing symphonies in the air. Our radio, a Super Heterodyne, the first radio on the Coast infuriated him and he refused to listen to it.

"You don't need radios," he said. "Why, I hear all the music I want to up in the Little Sur. There are symphonies in the air all the time."

One day he promised to bring me some marbles. I was excited, visualizing rainbow colored agates. To my great disappointment he arrived with a big bag of acorns.

"See all the lovely marbles," he said.

I was a polite child, having been carefully trained by my Victorian grandparents, so I thanked him. But I never played with them.

Al Clarke ate peas with a knife, and my mother often asked him to stay for dinner, invariably serving peas so that I could watch this fantastic performance. It was a real art not to drop a single one.

John Cooper III told me that Al Clarke quit working at the Cooper ranch because there wasn't enough Worchestershire sauce at the table!

"Al Clarke was a Harvard graduate," Doc Roberts went on. "And he had gone to the University of Edinburgh for his MA. He wound up at Columbia for his doctorate." But evidently something happened to him at Columbia which caused him to revolt against society.

"He told me," Doc Roberts continued, "That he was through with civilization. 'I reject everything,' he said. 'I shall go and get gold in California.'"

Some years later, Doc Roberts was amazed to run into him again in the Little Sur, then called Little River, where, by this time, he had become a hermit living in the wilderness, eating only vegetables that he got from the Cooper Ranch and wild honey. Occasionally he worked at the Cooper Ranch but most of the time he subsisted on what he could find in the wilderness. He was a strict vegetarian, and, during hunting season, protected the deer, whom he called by name. (Harry Vandal, over in Palo Colorado Canyon, did the same thing.)

He made Dr. Roberts promise to keep secret the fact that he was an educated man—entitled to use the appellation Dr. Clarke, or Albert Clarke, Ph.D.

After leaving Columbia, Clarke wound up in Monterey, where instead of searching for gold he embarked on a steady course of drinking until his money was gone. Then he wandered down the Coast and landed in the Little Sur. After a time he disappeared completely. He was gone for almost a year. The old timers thought he must have died in the back hills. Although he never told anyone where he went, not even his friend Doc Roberts, Doc felt certain that it was behind Pico Blanco.

He returned in the guise of a madman, claiming that he had found the secret of the gold but that it was wrong to use gold the way people use it. Gold was what was wrong with civilization. Since he had found the secret, he told Doc Roberts, he did not need to use it. If he used it, he lost it. In other words, the true value of the gold was its concept or essence, what might be termed its spiritual value. It possessed magical powers, such as crystals do. It had been misused for material purposes and mankind was paying the consequences of this.

Al Clarke knew where the Indian gold was hidden but would never use it or tell of it. He preferred to live without possessions, wandering around in the Little Sur, living on wild honey plus a rich gruel made of wheat and honey, and occupying himself taming the deer and giving them names. He could call each one to him individually.

"He was psychic," Doc Roberts repeated. "He always knew when I was coming.

"Do you really believe that?" I asked. "Or did he hear your car? There weren't very many cars coming down the old road and yours had a powerful engine." (It was an old Pierce Arrow.)

Doc Roberts paused and appeared to consider whether to go on or not.

"Many stranger things than that have happened," he said at last. "When I was first practicing down the Coast there was an Indian woman living in the Little Sur. She was a widow. She had a little boy, age nine, and he was ill. He had a seven year old sister. Every day the mother sent the sister on horseback down the road to get milk and the neighbors saw her going by with her brother behind her on the saddle. But her brother had been home sick in bed all the time."

"This was Indian magic," the mother claimed when Doc Roberts asked her about it. When it was needed, a person could send what the Egyptians would call his *ka* or etheric double in his stead, so that it could be seen by others. The boy was protecting his sister. (The Indian woman had never heard of the Egyptians, of course, but Doc Roberts had.)

No one who had seen the phenomenon could explain it but all claimed they had seen it with their own eyes. A neighbor saw the boy riding with his sister and thought he was well again, so she went to see the mother— and found the boy sick in bed.

"Yes, Al Clarke was psychic all right," Doc concluded. "Mine was not the only car coming down the only road—nor the only one with a powerful motor."

"Do you really think he found the secret of the Indian gold?" I asked.

Doc Roberts smiled. "Maybe he did."

"Don't forget," he said as I left, "to get it in the paper about my driving a horse and buggy down Alvarado Street. Everyone will think old Doc Roberts has gone dotty like old man Clarke."

He winked at me conspiratorially.

I left him, wondering about the Indian gold.

I kept my promise to put it in the newspaper although not on the front page and I was most disappointed that his son, Houghton, put a stop to his magnificent idea.

Doc Roberts' cabin, "Cyclone," in the Little Sur where he went to remember the days when he was a simple Coast doctor. In front of the cabin are his wife, née Edith Maltby, and her mother, Sarah Maltby. — Collection of John L.D. Roberts II

VII.

The Lost Indian Gold

*Robert Louis Stevenson ...came to Monterey in 1879 and visited the ruins of Carmel Mission with his beloved Fanny Osbourne. He set forth...to explore the Carmel sand dunes and marshy flats at the mouth of Carmel River, but without result. This search for lost treasure inspired him, however, to write **Treasure Island** whose setting was Point Lobos. Whaler's Knoll, which in 1879 was in use by the Portuguese and Azores Islanders whalers as a point for spotting whales, was the Spy Glass Mountain of Treasure Island.*

An ever lingering mystery down the Coast in early days was the whereabouts of the Indian gold. Although a rich vein of gold was found at Los Burros mine, south of Lucia, this was not the source of the Indian gold nor of the inexplicable gold dust they carried in quills. The mysterious gold dust had everyone puzzled from Spanish days on. No one was able to understand how it came to be in that form, unless it was collected from a dry steam bed high in the fastnesses of the Santa Lucias—the Ventana Primitive area.

Geologists and prospectors searched the mountains without success.

But in addition to gold dust, there was the Lost Mine of the Padres. From here rich gold in the form of nuggets was brought by the Indians to the Franciscan padres at Carmel Mission.

Not all the Indians were unhappy at Carmel Mission and there were those who were devoted to Father Serra.

However, the attitude of the Indians, even those who had completely embraced Christianity, remained ambivalent. They were willing to bring the fathers the precious gold from the mountains for their gold ornaments and chalices and gold plates but they refused to tell them where they got it. They said that they had sworn an oath of secrecy, never to reveal the secret to a white man. Neither the Rumsens nor the Esselens, traditional enemies that they were, would break this oath. (In any case, at the Mission, these former enemies had become brothers.)

When the pirate Hippolyte de Bouchard raided Carmel Mission in 1818, friendly Indians warned the Fathers of his advance, and in haste they buried the gold plate and other ornaments in the sands near the mouth of Carmel River. Bouchard, disappointed, found no gold at Carmel Mission.

Strangely, however, the precious gold ornaments and plates never reappeared—whether because the fathers and the Indians who hid them had forgotten their exact location or the tide had carried them out. Perhaps someone stole them. Nobody knows. The whole story is veiled in a mass of contradictory evidence and speculation.

Robert Louis Stevenson heard this tale when he came to Monterey in 1879 and visited the ruins of Carmel Mission with his beloved Fanny Osbourne. He set forth, in company with a Chinese man, to explore the Carmel sand dunes and marshy flats at the mouth of Carmel River, but without result. This search for lost treasure inspired him, however, to write *Treasure Island* whose setting was Point Lobos. Whaler's Knoll, which in 1879 was in use by the Portuguese and Azores Islanders whalers as a point for spotting whales, was the Spy Glass Mountain of *Treasure Island.*

Point Lobos, not far south of Carmel River, looked more like an island than like the little promontory that it was and there was an aura of mystery about it; it suggested to Stevenson the whole story, especially as it was said that pirates had landed there and used it as a base. (Highly improbable, as there is no place to land at Point Lobos; but of course they could have landed at Carmel River mouth and walked there.)

The brig *Star of the West* was wrecked at Lobos in the 1840s or 1850s and its valuable cargo salvaged by those who had wagons to carry it in, notably Captain J.B.R. Cooper who is said to have made a small fortune with it. The owner of the ill-fated vessel never recovered a penny. The ruling at the time was that "damaged goods" (from wrecked vessels) were public property and belonged to anyone who chose to haul them away.

No, Stevenson found no treasure on his treasure hunt, not in the form of gold, but it resulted in a classic which was more valuable than gold.

Ever since the secularization of the California Missions in 1834, people have made treks into the Santa Lucia mountains in search of the Lost Mine of the Padres. According to a story told me by James Ladd Delkin, publisher of the *Monterey Peninsula*, a guidebook compiled by the WPA writers' project, there was a city or rather a large *rancheria* near the lost mine inhabited by the Indians who worked there, and one day there was an avalanche or rock fall during a great storm when the wind raged from the South. The mine was buried along with the *rancheria* and all the Indians who were there at the time were killed. He did not tell me the source of this story but considered it authentic.

Some old timers think it may have been near the site of Camp Idlewild in the north fork of the Little Sur; others that it was on the south fork of the same river, or else behind Pico Blanco.

I said to the old timers, "Well, then, how come you haven't found the gold if you think you know where it is?"

"Oh well, we haven't had time to look for it."

A likely tale.

"Did you ever hear the legend that a white man would die if he looked for the Indian gold around Pico Blanco?"

They changed the subject.

On February 12, 1932, an account was given in the *Carmel Pine Cone*, a weekly newspaper, of an old Indian who knew the secret of the gold. In the article he was referred to as a Carmel Indian which probably meant he belonged to the Rumsen (or Carmelenyo) tribe, a branch of the so-called Costanoans, more recently called Olones.

José Barnabel, 104 year old picturesque Indian whose tribe once owned all of the Monterey Peninsula was buried this week, a pauper, whose only home for the past ten years has been a tent at Tortilla Flat. Bernabel is the last of the original tribe of Carmel Indians who roamed over this then primitive wilderness when Father Serra first came to California. He was at one time known throughout the state as a bronc buster.

Despite the fact that he died practically penniless, Bernabel could have been perhaps fabulously wealthy. Stories have been circulated in Carmel from time to time with some foundation that the aged Indian knew the definite location of the famous lost gold mine in the Big Sur district.

On several occasions, Bernabel was approached by gold prospectors who made alluring offers to him if he would reveal the secret. Bernabel's father is said to have been one of the Indians who brought huge nuggets of gold to the Padres in early days.

From his father, Bernabel learned the location of the missing mine on the promise that the secret should never be disclosed. True to his word, Bernabel died with his lips sealed although at times he had to beg for his food.

Bernabel was educated at Carmel Mission and during early days aided the Pades in their many activities. In the last ten years his only recreation was an occasional walk through Carmel with his dog as his companion.

Bernabel had a strong hatred of the white population and spoke but little English. Yet he had acquired from the Padres sufficient knowledge to speak Spanish fluently. He never attended a moving picture show or did he ever accept a ride in an automobile. He smoked a peculiar Indian weed which he would gather twice a year from the mountains surrounding Carmel.

> *The old Indian was stricken last week and*
> *neighbors telephoned Chief of Police Gus Englund*
> *who investigated. The officer found Bernabel*
> *almost unconscious, and the Indian was given*
> *medical aid by Dr. John Gray who ordered him to*
> *the County Hospital where he died.*

It was rumored that occasionally Bernabel returned from his treks into the Santa Lucias with gold dust as well as the weed he smoked, and sometimes gold nuggets. On this account, white men followed him into the mountains, but Bernabel cagily doubled on his tracks, thus evading his pursuers, and like an old fox, lost them.

A story about gold dust stored in quills was facetiously reported in the *Carmel Pine Cone* July 8, 1932.

> *Authors were not the only ones who used quills to*
> *keep the wolf from the door. It appears that Carmel*
> *Indians who resided in the Big Sur district had their*
> *own banking systems in the form of quills plucked*
> *from the tails of chickens. The quills were filled*
> *with gold dust and then deposited on ledges in a*
> *huge cave that is said to be ten miles south of*
> *Carmel and ten miles inland. This unique method*
> *of hiding money was disclosed for the first time by*
> *Thomas Morgan, veteran Monterey County*
> *pioneer. Morgan last week filed a gold claim and*
> *told County Recorder John E. Wallace of how the*
> *Indians had 'chicken a la king.'*

> *Morgan said he is making plans to search through*
> *his cave in the hope of finding several rows of*
> *quills that might have been overlooked by their*
> *long since defunct owners. According to Morgan,*
> *the Indians had no way of bankng their gold dust*
> *and for years it was their custom to hide it in quills.*

> *The more gold dust an Indian had, the less tail*
> *feathers had his chickens, so it was not difficult to*
> *gauge his wealth.*

This story, although written in a lightsome vein, was basically true—although the quills used were not necessarily chicken feathers but much more likely those of wild birds such as hawks, condors, herons or seagulls. Old timers down the Coast were always saying, "The Indians found gold whenever they ran out of money and they took it to town in the form of gold dust carried in quills." Many had actually seen these gold dust filled quills.

We first hear about gold dust carried in quills in early Spanish days. Indians from the Carmel Valley and the Sur Coast appeared in Monterey with quills filled with gold dust and traded them for the things they needed. They quickly learned that the white man valued the shining, precious metal. The profligate dons used the gold dust, when they had plenty of it, to stuff the Cascarone eggs at Monterey's annual Cascarone balls. To the tune of the traditional *varsoviana*, people danced on a floor glittering with the gold dust as well as confetti after the eggs had been broken over the heads of señoritas of the gentlemens' choice.

Inhabitants of Big Sur said that Mrs. Post knew the secret of the gold.

Josie Simonean Fussell, who at one time lived at Mill Creek in the house we occupied later, told me, "Whenever the Posts ran short of money, Mrs. Post would disappear for two or three days at a time and return with gold dust. She never told anyone where she got it."

She did not even tell her children about it, for, according to legend, the Indians were sworn not to reveal the secret to white men and her children were half-white.

It is also said that Sing Fat, the old Chinese man who used to collect seaweed in his spring wagon, was in reality using seaweed as a pretext for more lucrative activities. He had discovered the secret of the Indian gold and took it to town stored in quills; he also took silver dust stored in the same fashion.

To me the most fascinating story of all was told by Jess Artellan who had been born on the Cooper ranch in the Little Sur. "The gold was no secret to the people who lived in Little Sur in the 1890s," he said. Artellan himself knew where it was but had never gone after it because of the following legend.

"The gold was held by a spirit," Artellan related. "It was on a craggy ridge, in plain sight. It wasn't hidden. Lots of people knew about it. But they couldn't get near the gold for the spirit guarded it. Whenever they disturbed her territory, she appeared as a half spirit, divided in two, split down the middle. If you saw the other half, saw her in her entirety, death would result—or madness. She was a very beautiful woman—*muy blanco,"* Artellan said, which is to say she was white skinned with golden hair. "When people got close to the gold she came down from the headwaters, over the falls. If people didn't stop when they saw her, something happened to them. Only Indians could get near."

Artellan had no Indian blood; he was half French, half Spanish.

John Roberts II believed that old man Clarke had actually found the gold and met the spirit who guarded it and that was why he was seemingly mad. She had punished him for pursuing the path towards the gold.

When John was six years old, he went down to *Cyclone,* his grandfather's rustic cabin in the Little Sur, and he and his grandfather met Al Clarke as usual, shouting as he came down the canyon.

He said to Dr. Roberts, "I knew you would have your

grandson with you this time.   I have something for him.
Please excuse us.   We're going down by the river."

He said to the boy, "You're a good friend.   Your grandfather is
my most favored friend."

He opened one of the little bags he had brought with him and
pulled out stones.   One was a round stone like an agate.   Others
may have been bits of gold ore and some gold dust.

He said, "Please tell no one I have given you this.   I like your
grandfather very much, so you
must be wealthy."   Then he
opened his other little bag.   "This
is mine.   This is much better
wealth than what I have given
you."

There were small ordinary
stones and some earth in the
bag; also some mica or "fool's
gold."

"This is mine," he repeated.
"No one else can ever get it
away from me and no one else
can go and get the other gold
now."

John L.D. Roberts II, Doc's grandson, was a little
boy when old man Clarke took him down to the
Little Sur River and revealed to him the
mysterious secret of the gold—"the root of all
evil."   —Collection of John L.D. Roberts II

Then he put the stones, earth,
mica, gold dust and sand back
into the little bags and
admonished, "Don't tell your grandfather."

Had he shown the six-year-old some real gold that he had
found in the north fork of Little Sur above the waterfall where
the spirit guarded it?   No one will ever know.

Redwood tree at Rainbow Lodge where George Sterling, the poet, made a swing for the Hogue children. Later, as it hung, frayed, people thought it a hangman's rope and the tree became known as a Hangman's Tree.　　　　　　　　　　　　　—Postcard.

VIII.

The Robinson Jeffers Coast

George Sterling, the poet, ...had settled in Carmel in 1906, just after the San Francisco earthquake and brought with him a group of writers, all of whom belonged to the famed Bohemian Club that met at Coppa's Restaurant. Among them were Jack London, Ambrose Bierce, Jimmy Hopper, Mary Austin and Nora May French. Later comers... included William Rose Benét, Sinclair "Red" Lewis, Upton Sinclair, Michael Williams, Kathleen and George Norris, Frederick Bechdolt, Alice McGowan and her sister Grace McGowan Cooke and Jesse Lynch Williams.

R obinson Jeffers made his first trip down the Coast to Big Sur on December 24, 1914. World War I had started and he and his wife, Una, had recently arrived from Santa Barbara with their big English bull dog, Billy Road, and rented a log house on Monteverde Street not far from Mary Austin's famous treehouse where she perched and wrote. It was George Sterling, the poet, who had enticed Jeffers into coming to Carmel. George Sterling had settled there in 1906, just after the San Francisco earthquake and brought with him a group of writers, all of whom belonged to the famed Bohemian Club that met at Coppa's Restaurant. Among them were Jack London, Ambrose Bierce, Jimmy Hopper, Mary Austin and Nora May French. (The latter was a poetess who committed suicide at the age of 26. She was in love with George Sterling who did not return her affections; she offered him a poisoned sandwich at a picnic, then snatched it and ate it herself.) Later comers, who had arrived in 1910 after the burning of Helican Hall, a Socialist community in the New Jersey Palisades, included William Rose Benét, Sinclair "Red" Lewis, Upton Sinclair, Michael Williams, Kathleen and George Norris, Frederick Bechdolt, Alice McGowan and her sister Grace McGowan Cooke (they wrote pulp love stories in collaboration) and Jesse Lynch Williams whose play, *Why Marry?* won the first Pulitzer prize in 1921.

George Sterling was the only member of the little writers' group aside from Jimmy Hopper who was interested in the Coast to the south. He went on numerous expeditions afoot or on horseback, getting to know the people who lived there and hearing their tales. He stopped in at the old Gilkey house at Mill Creek, by this time the Hogue ranch house, and found that the three Hogue children, Ruth, Elizabeth and Dean, had no swing; so next time he went down on horseback he took a long stout rope and a board to be used as a seat for the swing. He attached the rope, by pulley, to an ancient redwood tree close to the house. For years after the Hogue children left for

Bixby Mountain and we occupied the place, the old rope still hung from the tree—also the swing, but it hung crookedly and the rope was badly frayed. Passersby, looking for lurid tales, thought the tree was a hangman's tree and the rope a hangman's rope. My mother never disabused them of this notion. On the contrary, she encouraged it and, if I remember correctly, even manufactured similar tales.

Robinson Jeffers, the poet who put the Sur Coast on the map; indeed his work became synonymous with it. He did not achieve world renown however until Judith Anderson talked him into writing *Medea* for her, and it hit Broadway.
— Courtesy of the Carmel Library

The entire Coast fascinated Sterling. He took Ambrose Bierce down with him once, but Bierce didn't enjoy it. He found it rough and uncomfortable and refused to repeat the experience. Jimmy Hopper, on the other hand, loved to go down the old road on horseback, and went often, but not with Sterling, as Sterling had moved away.

Sterling's enthusiastic, lyrically descriptive letters to Jeffers, describing the Sur and its isolated inhabitants, struck a chord and after the Jeffers lost their first child, Maeve, they moved to Carmel where he and Una walked down to Ocean Avenue on December 20, 1914, and took the horse-drawn mail stage that left before dawn and arrived at Pfeiffer's Resort in the Big Sur by dark.

George Sterling, the poet, and Jimmy Hopper — members of the early writer's colony at Carmel in 1906. It was Sterling who induced Robinson Jeffers to come to Carmel and explore the Coast to the south.

—Courtesy of Elayne Hopper Chanslor

Corbett Grimes was the mail stage driver, as fate would have it, and he was a garrulous young man recently arrived from Liverpool who was later to become known as the Coast's best story teller. He had come to visit his uncle, Ed Grimes, who had married Ellen Post, at his ranch on the high trail below Big Sur, and he was all agog with the wonders of the place which exceeded anything he had ever heard in England of the wonders of the Wild West. On their way down the Coast, Grimes regaled his fascinated passengers with dramatic tales, pointing out every landmark where an accident, murder, suicide, or lynching had occurred.

Naturally he gave Jeffers the impression that the Coast was all violence, all somberness and brooding.

Going down Little Sur grade, Jeffers and his bull dog, Billy Road, had to get out and walk because of the weight in the wagon. Corbett was carrying a full load of supplies as well as bags of mail. Grimes pointed out a deserted cabin, not far from the road, where a man had died a few years earlier after returning to the Sur after a trip to San Francisco where he had been shanghaied. He was so glad to be free that he died happy. But now his cabin had fallen into rack and ruin.

They arrived at Pfeiffer's just after dark and found that Mrs. Pfeiffer was away. "John Pfeiffer had made the bread," Jeffers told me. "He got onions in it. And the bread was very oniony."

I asked Jeffers what his first impression of the Coast was on that wintry day. "The Coast seemed solitary; there was a light rain. I would not have written the same kind of thing if it had been a different kind of landscape. My first impression of the Coast: it was winter time, darker and more sinister. I was shocked later when I saw the Big Sur in summer and the hills golden. Perhaps I shouldn't have said sinister; rather hostile to its inhabitants."

Corbett Grimes was the garrulous stage driver who told the Jeffers dramatic tales on their first trip to the Sur on December 20, 1914. Here he is shown with his daughter "Toots" (Mary).   — Photo by author

"People have treated the landscape so badly in America," he added.

After the first trip with Corbett Grimes, the Jeffers went down once or twice a year; their first trip on a motor-drawn stage was in 1923.

I then asked Jeffers about his characters, whether he had ever based them on the actual people of the Sur Coast.

"The only people I ever put in a story were Mary Van Wingt and her husband Charlie Van Wingt. Charlie was working for Harry Leon Wilson. He was a Dutchman. After he married Mary, an Indian woman, somebody asked him, 'I hear you got married, Charlie,' 'Oh, not as bad as all that.' But it *was* as bad as all that," said Jeffers, twinkling.

The Roan Stallion was suggested by a deserted farm house he came upon in San Jose Creek where he heard someone had been killed by a stallion. He used Mary—or Indian Mary as she was called in the village of Carmel—as the model for California of the poem. But in reality Jeffers didn't know or even talk to Mary.

"I saw her driving around in an old buggy."

The extraordinary thing was that in real life, unbeknownst to Jeffers, Indian Mary had actually been involved with a stallion. In the poem, the Indian woman, California, lived in the hills above Mal Paso Creek, just south of Carmel, and was married to a brutal white husband. She fell in love with a stallion who symbolized, to Jeffers, God or "the inhuman magnificence of things." It was the opposite of what he called "racial introversion," whose symbol was incest in the tragic poems. In the end, California, "moved by some obscure human fidelity," shot to death the beautiful stallion when he was about to trample to death her drunken husband.

Jeffers was astonished that afternoon at Tor House when I had tea with him and Una prior to the publication of the *Double Axe,* when I told him that Indian Mary had indeed been involved with a stallion, although not in the way California was. When Indian Mary was 16, her brothers gave her a stallion. One day, when Mary was away from home, they sold him to a neighbor. Mary was heartbroken. The stallion's name was Boola. She went to work for the neighbor to earn back the stallion, and had almost paid the debt when Boola ran away. Mary searched for him in the hills and canyons, tearing her hands and clothes in the mesquite, calling, "Boola, Boola," and at last she found him in a swamp, unable to extricate himself. He was fast sinking and had a broken leg.

Tor House, built by the poet out of hand-hewn native granite hauled up from the beach below. Contrary to popular belief, Hawk Tower was not built as a place to write but as a play-room for his twin sons.   —Courtesy of the Carmel Library

Mary took out her gun and shot him.

How did Jeffers know this? He didn't. But he had somehow intuited Mary's connection with a stallion—enough to provide him unconsciously with the germ of a theme.

Jeffers was a very intuitive man.

There was no denying the fact that Corbett Grimes' lurid tales had influenced him greatly on his first visit to the Coast on that winter's day in 1914, however.

"The first time I went down to Serra Hill," he went on, "There were lots of buckeye trees. Grimes marked the spot where a wagon load of corpses fell over the side. The corpses rolled down the hill. Corbett said he didn't know if they retrieved them all."

The corpses were from the wreck of the *S.S. Ventura* in 1873. Grimes also pointed out a deserted cabin on the road opposite Doc Roberts' place, *Cyclone*, where a woman had hanged herself and her four children after being deserted by her lover who had worked on the old county road.

The somberness of that day was never entirely to fade from Jeffers' mind despite subsequent impressions.

In *Tamar*, the first of his tragic poems to use incest as a theme and in which he "sheared off the rhyme tassels from his verse," Jeffers, however, did refer to an actual incident which had received widespread attention in the press.

In *Tamar* a man named Verdugo had been killed at a shack in a gum tree grove near the mouth of San Jose Creek by Sylvia Vierra and her man. The three of them had gotten drunk on red wine and the woman thought Verdugo was abusing her nine year old daughter. They killed him with a big kitchen knife, then put his body on a bonfire. The next day Tamar Caldwell, in the poem, saw a man's foot hanging out of the fire, found the couple drunkenly asleep in the shack and the child crying. She took the child away.

This, with altered names, bore a distinct resemblance to the truth. It was Jimmy Hopper, famed short story writer and athlete,   a war correspondent during World War I and a member of Carmel's original writer's colony, who told me the actual tale. It was he who had written the story of the trial in the *San Francisco Call Bulletin.*

"There was an Indian in Carmel named José Peralta," Jimmy Hopper told me. "He was very natty and wore a sombrero with a feather. He walked lightly and was built graceful as a cat. One day I was chopping wood. He came in the yard and stood behind me. 'How well you chop,' he said. He was a bit drunk. 'Mr. Hopper could you give me a glass of port?' "I haven't any,' I told him. 'Mr. Sterling, he always used to give me a little glass of port.' He kept standing there, smiling, 'Goodbye, Mr. Hopper." he said. The next day, on the road towards Lobos, there were two girls herdng cattle. They saw a fire burning there. It was a dangerous fire. They went to look at it and saw a human foot sticking out of the fire. They looked into the little shack. José Peralta and a Mexican girl were sleeping peacefully together. They had a picnic the night before with Charlie Escobar. Everyone got drunk on red wine. Charlie got in a fight with José and got stabbed. Who stabbed him? Both José and the Mexican girl had been quite drunk. 'Let's build a bonfire and put him on it' they said hazily. Hours later they were still asleep and the body still burning. At the trial the question arose as to whether José or the girl had done the actual stabbing. They couldn't remember."

The shack burned to the ground. José Peralta went to jail on a manslaughter charge; the Mexican girl was let off on probation.

And the child? Yes, there had been one but Jimmy Hopper didn't want to talk about it. She was still living and he wanted to conceal her identity.

It was the Allen girls, the daughters of Alexander M. Allen, who owned Point Lobos, Margaret and Eunice, who found the body.

Jeffers did admit to basing the character Fayne Fraser in *Give Your Heart to the Hawks* on the red-haired wife of a lighthouse keeper at Point Sur—but he knew nothing about her beyond that.

My father, he explained, was *not* the model for the mean old rancher in the *Loving Shepherdess.* "His character was totally imaginary." he said.

"But your father disliked me," Jeffers went on, "because he got me mixed up with George Sterling and we were both poets. George went down there with a gun and was going to go hunting on your father's property. Your father was furious. He hated me because he thought I was George."

This was not the only reason, however. Although my father was a Greek scholar who enjoyed reading Euripides, Sophocles, Aeschylus (but the comic Aristophanes was his favorite), he failed to perceive the relationship between Greek tragedy and Jeffers' classic themes. He did not understand Jeffers' symbolism. He thought his mention of incest outrageous and that all of his work was degenerate and ought to be burned. And it *was* being burned at the time in huge bonfires by people who thought as my father did. It was kept on the locked shelves of libraries along with Rabelais and the Marquis de Sade. This was true even in Jeffers' hometown, Carmel, until *Thurso's Landing* came out. Then all the poems were made available to the public; *The Roan Stallion,* in particular, raised an enormous furor.

Another thing that annoyed my father about Jeffers was that tourists confused the Sharpe family with the protagonists of the poems. Not only did they think my father was the mean old rancher who refused shelter to the dying Shepherdess in *The Loving Shepherdess* but that my mother was the prototype of the violet-eyed Helen Thurso who had killed her paralyzed husband with bichloride of mercury tablets. (Helen had fallen in love with a construction worker on the new highway, Rick Armstrong.) Since our house was obviously the Thurso ranch house, tourists flocked down our hill in droves and stopped in at Rainbow Lodge to ask my mother, "Are you Helen?"

Mother's stock reply, delivered dead-pan, was, "If I were, I wouldn't have used bichloride of mercury tablets."

Bichloride of mercury tablets were used in the 1930s to induce abortions. My mother's strange remark startled and baffled the tourists who scuttled off without further questions.

Our neighbor, Florence Hogue, was so angry with Jeffers because she thought he had based one of his heroines on her daughter Ruth that she talked of suing him.

Jeffers as he said himself, was deeply influenced by the land which became his locale, but in reality it was an extraordinary conjunction of locale and man; for without Jeffers the landscape could never have been voiced in the way it was and without the landscape he could never have found his own true voice. His themes were classical, timeless and always symbolic; this was the point so many people missed.

I shall never forget the afternoon in 1947 at Tor House, with Una darting in and out serving tea and interspersing apropos remarks, such as how much more vivid and poignant the landscape was when one saw an old cartwheel or calla lilies growing on the site of a vanished door-step; the human element was, thus, brought into contrast with the inhuman and became very alive. The fire was burning in the fireplace and the sea crashing outside. I said to Jeffers, "You seem to always depict a conflict between man and nature, a split between them, a deep antogonism between."

"I'm more on the side of the landscape," Jeffers quickly

admitted, with a glint in his intense blue eyes and an infectious grin.

"What about humanity?" I asked.

"There's hope for humanity and it will go on for a long time to come," he told me. "If an atom bomb wrecked civilization it wouldn't kill all the people."

"And what should people do?"

"Live along decently. I don't think the race is improving. But cruelty is the only form of wickedness I know of. Extreme dishonesty is sort of contemptible; not wicked."

We had ended our interview for the newspaper (it was about the forthcoming *Double Axe* so none of the material in this chapter has been published previously) and now we went on to talk about ghosts, nature spirits, Ella Young, etc.

Ella Young was the extraordinary Irish woman for whom Noel Sullivan had created a seat in Celtic lore at U.C. Berkeley where she lectured on Gaelic mythology and spoke of nature spirits, fairies, elves, pixies and the like.

"To me the great thing about Ella Young was not the psychic thing," Jeffers remarked, "but her wit." He also was impressed by her compassion, and described a time when he, Una and Ella Young were driving down the Coast road and a rattlesnake was crossing the road. Ella insisted on Una's stopping the car, and she got out, picked up the rattlesnake and carried it to safety. It did not strike her.

Jeffers was particularly interested in the ghosts (or stories of ghosts) he had encountered in Ireland when he was writing *Descent to the Dead*. "One of them stank to high heaven," he told me, "and thus announced his presence."

Una Call Jeffers, the poet's great love and source of inspiration. In an Arnold Genthe photo.
—Courtesy Bancroft Library

We agreed that one of the remarkable things about the Sur Coast was the absence of ghosts, except for Indian ghosts. (He, like myself, was ever aware of the Indian presence there.) Then he went on to tell me of "the little dark people" that John Steinbeck's mother saw in the Big Sur when she was teaching school there in the 1890s.

I, too, had seen them, as had Susan Porter of Coastlands and Armine von Tempski, the red-haired Hawaiian novelist who had written *Born in Paradise* in addition to many novels about Hawaii. Armine saw them at Point Lobos.

I thought of the "dark watchers" in Steinbeck's classic short story, *"Flight."*

"Did Steinbeck believe in the little dark people?" I asked.

I needn't have asked. Jeffers and I did and we were certain that Steinbeck did. Steinbeck's close friend Ed Rickets, the "Doc" of Steinbeck's *Cannery Row*, had also told me of seeing "the little dark people."

Jeffers merely grinned.

Bixby Landing when still in operation in 1911. Here cargo such as barrels of lime and, earlier, tanbark and lumber, were lowered by trestle to the waiting holds of ships anchored offshore.
—Collection of Frank Trotter

IX.

Rainbow Lodge

Down in the clearing in Mill Creek Canyon stood the old Gilkey ranch house, painted a deep rose color with an orange-yellow roof, a color I have never seen on a ranch house before or since.

M y father bought the 300 acre ranch at Mill Creek in 1919, soon after the end of World War I. He was a regular Army officer who retired young due to service incurred disabilities, but he had returned to active duty during World War I as an instructor at an officer's training school in Corvallis, Oregon, where his father, a retired Colonel, was commanding officer. My father, who had run away to serve in the Spanish-American war at the age of 17, had graduated from Dartmouth but he had always wanted to be a writer. So he became a reporter on the Denver Post where his father, at the time, was on the teaching staff of the University of Colorado. But my father's wild ways, such as drinking and keeping a red-haired mistress, caused his father to persuade (nay command) him to accept a commission in the Army. He continued to write during the course of his Army career under the pen-name Alfred D. Pettibone. His adventure novels about Army life were published serially in *Argosy Adventure Magazine* along with Jackson Gregory and Edgar Rice Burroughs. Jack London, too, occasionally appeared in *Argosy* and my father's style was often compared to London's. His work also appeared in the *Railroad Magazine* and in *American Detective*. Much of his published work, however, was done after his retirement in 1913, when he had all of his time to devote to writing; yet he never tired of telling of the joy of writing novels "with bullets whizzing through my tent."

My parents first lived in New York, after his retirement, then in Sausalito until America entered the war. I was born at the end of 1918, soon after the Armistice. My father was still in uniform when he bought the ranch.

My father had been stationed at the Presidio of Monterey when he met and married my mother in 1911 and he had never forgotten the beauty of the area and of the wild Coast to the south. He wanted to find a place in the country to settle down and write. He parked my mother and me, the baby, with his parents in Redlands where my grandfather was President of the Orange Growers Association, then came up to explore the Coast below Carmel.

He found what seemed to him to be the perfect place at Mill Creek, where three ill-assorted partners, who had bought it from the Hogues, were unsuccessfuly trying to run a tourist resort. It was beautiful. There was a beach and a mile and a half of trout stream. Mountains rose on every side overshadowing the old 1870s ranch house. He loved it. He wrote my mother, "I want this place more than I ever wanted anything in my life."

Capt. Howard G. Sharpe, retired. As he appeared when he bought the ranch at Mill Creek in 1919, just after the Armistice. At the ranch he sometimes wore old Army dungarees, at other times golfing knickers.
—Collection of author

She wrote back, "Buy it."

She had no idea of how isolated it was, nor how primitive; she visualized, she told me later, a little place such as one found at Pebble Beach with steps leading down to the sea and a staff of tried and true family retainers who looked after the place when one went away. This picture was the antithesis of the truth.

She was, she told me when I was grown, utterly appalled when my father drove her down the Coast in his Model T Ford pointing out the wonders of the landscape. All she could see was the horrendous wagon road, dangerously overhanging precipices, with no places to turn around and few places to pass and worst of all the huge mountains that overshadowed the ranch house. (Mother was claustrophobic.)

But she decided to grit her teeth and bear it.

The limekiln at Mill Creek when still in operation. It closed down in 1911 when a log-jam caused a flood. Most of the people who lived there moved out, including the Fussells, and West Smith closed his bar.   — Collection of Frank Trotter

"Yes," she assented, every time my father pointed out another beauty of the landscape. Later she came to love it but she was horrified at first sight.

In 1919 the Coast was quiet and sparsely populated, much as it had been in the 1870s before the industrial boom. The industries which had brought hundred of lumberjacks, millhands, limekiln workers and miners into the country in the 1880s, 1890s, and early 1900s had shut down, leaving in their wake a litter of crumbling shacks and barns, rotting lime barrels, abandoned mine shafts and ruined boat landings. At Mill Creek the fireblackened trestles that had once supported an aerial tramway from the Limekiln (the Monterey Lime Company) three miles up the canyon to Bixby Landing hung like skeletal fingers and lent a ghostly, even a sinister touch to the scene. (A forest fire had left the trestles blackened.) Bixby Landing, too, was in an abandoned state. The old brick oven that had fueled the cables that lowered cargo down to the holds of waiting ships was still there as were mounds of rotting lime barrels; and there was also an old Japanese shack, complete with built-in wooden bedstead and wooden pillow racks, for many Japanese worked at the Limekiln in addition to Italians.

Down in the clearing in Mill Creek Canyon stood the old Gilkey ranch house, painted a deep rose color with an orange-yellow roof, a color I have never seen on a ranch house before or since. In addition there were numerous out-buildings, a barn, a corral, a dance hall, a

Rainbow Lodge—house, barn, dance-hall, cabins, numerous outbuldings—as it appeared when my father bought it in 1919. The old wagon road can be seen wandering up Serra Hill to the South.
—Collection of author

stable, and several cabins which were rented to tourists. The ranch came equipped with six horses. My father had great dreams for the place. He named it Rainbow Lodge. He put running water in the house, a kitchen sink, and a bathroom with a flush toilet, washbasin and a bath tub—things which had never been seen on this primitive Coast before. He also built a garage for his Model T Ford, a country store, a gas pump for the tourists who came during the summer time, and, in his initial enthusiasm, turned to various agricultural endeavors—a fruit orchard, a chicken yard and chicken houses, rabbits and rabbit hutches, a vegetable garden and he planted five acres of potatoes in the big field below the house. He also bought a Jersey cow to provide milk for me, the baby, and for butter, cheese, cottage cheese and cream. He made a deal with our closest neighbor, Tony Brazil on Serra Hill, to breed the cow once a year to one of his best bullls; if it was a heifer it would be ours; but a bull calf would go to the Brazils. For some peculiar reason, Bossy, the cow, produced only bull calves and they all went to the Brazils. We didn't learn until

The ranch house at Rainbow Lodge.   Built in 1875 and successively occupied by the Gilkeys, Fussells, Hogues and Sharpes. Frida Sharpe tore it down in 1934 so she wouldn't have to live here anymore.   —Collection of Frank Trotter

years later that the Sharpes were the laughing stock of the Coast. "Why, those city folk don't even know the difference between a bull calf and a heifer calf!"

My father's agricultural endeavors, in general, seemed cursed, mainly due to his inexperience. The gophers got all five acres of potatoes; my father didn't know one was supposed to put wire netting under the soil to keep them out and no one told him. A fire burned down the fruit orchard. My father, who was afraid of horses due to a horse accident on the Parade ground years earlier, didn't keep the stables up properly. One night my mother went and let all six horses out to wander on the road—and our neighbors fell heir to them except for one old mare who kept wandering back and forth along the road, grazing as she went. She was too old to ride or be bred. Then, one winter when the entire family was down with pneumonia and my mother the only one on her feet (and no hired help), she let the chickens and rabbits out. She didn't have time to tend them. I suppose the foxes and coyotes got them. Only the vegetable garden was successful, and Bossy, the cow, became our pet, accompanying us on every walk in the woods along with our two dogs, Carlo, the shepherd, and Roddy, the collie, plus our red rooster and the cat, Lady Gray. What a procession!

During the day Bossy grazed up on the Mesa, then she would get to the top of the trail and bawl for someone to come and get her. We had to do it although she was perfectly capable of coming down the trail herself.

My father, who had been a surveyor and done a lot of engineering in the Army, took to road building and bridge building, not to mention trails and finding springs to turn into water supplies. He built a road up the canyon, another one down to the beach. There were numerous camp sites for tourists, complete with elegant out-houses, and he added several cabins so that there was a total of seven (if one included my two-room playhouse, which was as big as the rest.)

Frida Grace Sharpe. A noted beauty—both in her native Santa Clara and in Monterey where she taught school in 1911.   —Photo by Bianca Conti

The tourist season at Rainbow Lodge was a short one. They came only in the summer time when school was out. Immediately after Labor Day, traffic stopped completely. Not a horn was to be heard on the old county road until the following May or June. The mail stage, however, came down three times a week. One day it drove to Pfeiffer's Resort in the Big Sur; the next day it returned again. In early days at the ranch, it was drawn by horses, but in 1923, the year my brother William ("Beans") was born, the spring wagon was replaced by a motorized vehicle. In the winter, however, during the storm and slide season, the mail had to be carried on horseback. Its two main ports of call were at our place, the Sur post office, and at Arborlado at the Post's ranch. (Later Arborlado post office moved to the Big Sur.)

The winters were lonely, hard and cold at the ranch, and the ranch house was darkened by the shadows of the mountains by 3 o'clock in the afternoon at which time we lit the kerosene lamps and built the fire in the wood stove.

I remember my childhood with the usual ambivalence. Part was beautiful; part was the antithesis, and there was always violence and terror. My father, evidently due to his war-service, had a case of what was later called "shell-shock." He was a very bad tempered man, always shouting, threatening, and issuing orders. He ordered the hired men around as though they were privates. And the hired men, alas, were almost always dangerous fellows. It was hard to get help in this lonely country; no one would respond to an ad; so my father took to hiring them off the county road as they came walking through carrying bundles on their backs. Many of these bindle stiffs were ex-cons, bums, hop-heads, murderers on parole and I.W.W.s. They took this road under the delusion that it was a short cut between Monterey and San Luis Obispo. It looked that way on the map. They failed to notice that the glorified wagon road (and it was just that, despite the annual county scrapers and graders) ended at Post's beyond Big Sur and below that there was nothing but trail—and a hundred miles of it at that.

One such drifter was Kelly.

Kelly worked for us eleven days.

Father met Kelly on his way home from town. It was getting on towards dark when he saw him with a bundle on his back on the road past Carmel Highlands.

"Where are you going?" asked Father.

"San Luis Obispo" said Kelly out of the corner of his mouth. (This betrayed the fact that he was an ex-con.)

"Why, you'll never get there," Father told him. "There's

nothing but trail beyond Post's. It's over 100 miles. You'd starve to death. Lots of men have died on that trail. Why don't you stop at my ranch and chop wood? I'll give you room and board and a dollar a day."

"Okay," said Kelly.

A dollar a day with room and board was good wages in the early 1920s, especially as there were so few jobs around for bindle-stiffs and ex-cons; and Kelly had nothing to lose. He was headed for nowhere.

In early winter the days were getting shorter; the rainy season was about to begin and there was plenty of wood to be chopped. Already the fires had to be lighted by 3 p.m. Otherwise dampness and pneumonia would set in.

My mother distrusted Kelly at first glance.

"You'd better fire Kelly," she said to my father at dinner.

"Why he's no worse than others who have worked here," my father said. "We've had lots of murderers, ex-cons, and hop-heads. He's no worse than the rest."

Mother said nothing more. She knew it was useless to argue. She also knew it was merely a matter of time before something happened.

She fed Kelly quantities of corn meal mush, for which, it appeared, he had a devouring passion, and it seemed to keep him quiet. But the atmosphere was tense in the house. I could feel it, although I was only six. My mother warned me to be careful of Kelly, not to talk to him or draw attention to myself. This was hard to do when he was painting the walls of my nursery bedroom—but Mother came in and told me to play outdoors.

On the eleventh day, my father said to Kelly at breakfast, "Well Kelly, it looks as if we've got enough wood chopped to hold us for awhile. Today we'll do some dynamiting. Got to get that road to the beach opened up. Can't do it after it starts to rain."

Father was building a road down to the beach and in the section he called the Narrows, about a quarter of a mile from the beach, there was a big outcropping of granite that had to be blasted.

"I wish you wouldn't dynamite today," Mother said.

"Oh, pshaw," said my father. "If I wait till it starts to rain, it'll be too late. It might not quit raining for a month. We have to do it today."

A few minutes later, the two men started down the canyon on foot with caps and fuses.

The beach was nearly a mile from the house, so Mother knew it would take them about 15 or 20 minutes to reach their destination at the Narrows. She hadn't much time.

As soon as they left, she packed a suitcase, got us children dressed in our town clothes, and put on her tailored tweed suit and Knox hat. Then she told me and my two-year-old brother, William, to be very, very quiet and to hide in the nursery; we were not to move or say anything no matter what happened. There was a little closet where she kept her sewing machine and when the door was closed no one noticed its existence.

"If you hear any commotion, hide in there," she told us, "and don't make a sound."

Although I was only six, my brother two, we were used to

obeying orders unquestioningly. Not only was father a military man, but in addition there was no time for explanations when one lived in a country where an eagle might swoop down (they were said to sometimes bear small children away in their talons) or a mountain lion might attack or a rattlesnake strike without an instant's warning. Obedience was mandatory. We learned that very young.

Mother got out the loaded cane my grandfather, Colonel Alfred C. Sharpe, had given her and sat down on the porch to wait in the Philippine throne chair. The loaded cane was a lethal weapon, as effective as a gun.

She knew only one man was coming back, but she didn't know which one.

It was a long, tense wait.

Less than an hour had passed when she heard a step at the back door—the kitchen door. Then she heard someone coming through the kitchen.

The loaded cane came across her knees, her hand upon it. She picked it up and aimed it at the door that would shortly open.

Then she heard a sniff.

My father had catarrh, so she knew it was my father. She put down the loaded cane. My father entered, looking white.

"What happened?" Mother asked.

"Why, Kelly's dead," he told her. "He blew off his head with a stick of dynamite and tried to kill me at the same time."

When the two men had got down to the Narrows, my father started telling Kelly how to do the dynamiting. Kelly hated being given orders and my father was used to giving them.

"I've done lots of dynamiting," Kelly said truculently. "I know about it."

"Well," said my father, "go ahead then. Only take plenty of fuse. That's one thing we've got plenty of. I'll walk down canyon and you walk up canyon after you light the fuse."

But he didn't like the way Kelly was handling the dynamite. He started down canyon before Kelly had lighted the fuse and had gone only a few paces when there was a terrific explosion. Flying rocks hit him in the back, knocking him down but not injuring him. He picked himself up and turned around to see Kelly, standing grotesquely, with the top of his head blown off and one eye hanging clear down to his chest.

"I knew Kelly was dead," Father said. "I'd seen plenty of dead men. But it was awful to see him still standing with his eye hanging down like that."

Kelly toppled and fell. Father went over and listened for his heart beat. There was none.

At this exact moment it began to rain.

Father walked up canyon to the house.

Mother said, "Well, you'd better go back down canyon and stand guard over the body until we get help. I'll try to flag down a car."

It was unlikely that a car would appear so late in the season but there was nothing else to do. The only telephone in the country was at Point Sur Lighthouse, over six miles to the south over the winding wagon road. For some reason Mother thought it proper that Father should guard the body instead of driving to town to summon help. On the other hand, there was always the possibility that wild animals might prey upon the body of the dead man.

Miraculously a car turned up only half an hour later. Mother flagged it down and asked the people to drive to Point Sur Lighthouse to phone the Coroner. Later that afternoon, the Coroner's black wagon appeared and the men walked down canyon with a stretcher to relieve my father, still standing in the rain by Kelly's mutilated body. It had been a gruesome vigil.

Kelly's body was taken to town and an inquest was held. The verdict was accidental death. However, it seemed clear that the man had, in reality, committed suicide and attempted to murder my father at the same time. He had cut the fuse short.

In his pockets they found an I.W.W. card and an empty wallet. The only money he had in the world was the $11.00 wages my father owed him.

My father was a bit leery of bindle-stiffs after that, but still there was little choice in this lonely country. Nobody wanted to work there. There were no bars, no movies, no women, no poker games, nothing to do on a Saturday night. The dance hall at Rainbow Lodge had never been opened; Father tore it down and used the lumber to build a cabin.

Much of the trouble at our ranch was due to the hired help. When I was a baby we had a crazy Chinese cook who sometimes went into manic rages, threatening everyone with a butcher knife. Mother found that the sight of a baby would calm him, so every time he got into one of his rages and brought forth his butcher knife, she took me into the kitchen; he quieted down and chucked me under the chin.

Then there were the two hired men who were sharing a cabin

down by the creek and one night they got drunk on canned heat (Sterno.) The bigger of the two men came up to the house in the middle of the night, pounding on the front door and crying, "Mrs. Sharpe, Mrs. Sharpe, let me in. Sam is going to kill me."

Mother was alone at the ranch. My father had blood poisoning and his father, the retired Colonel, had come down from Palo Alto to drive him up to Letterman Hospital. As he left, my grandfather gave her a gun and told her to always carry it at her hip and to sleep with it under her pillow. "Under no circumstances," he admonished her, "let anyone into the house at night, especially not the hired men."

But Charlie sounded so terrified that she hadn't the heart to refuse him, and she let him sleep in the living room on the sofa.

The next morning the trouble had blown over; the effect of the canned heat had worn off. The two hired men again became the best of friends and went back to work on Father's road to the beach where they were, by this time, building a bridge.

Our favorite hired man was a Danish murderer on parole; he had shot a man up in the north of California for killing his pet dog and been put in jail for it. We knew he was going to someday escape for Denmark. He left one day and we did not report it to the authorities as we were supposed to do.

A few months later, we received a postcard from Copenhagen telling us of the beauties of the landscape there, so my parents knew he had made it safely. We never reported this either. I remember him clearly although I could not have been four. He had clear, beautiful eyes and told wonderful stories about Denmark. Sometimes he told me the tales of Hans Christian Andersen. He was kind to children and was, indeed, a gentle soul.

A hired man of another sort was paranoid. He said he had a military secret (a weapon, we supposed) of the greatest importance to all world governments. All were pursuing him which was why he was hiding out at our place. He mistrusted all the tourists who stopped there, insisting that they were spies. He said that patriotism told him he should give the secret to the United States, but that other governments were bidding higher. He didn't know what to do. One day he packed up and disappeared down the road. That was the last we heard of him.

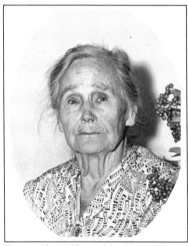

Florence Young Hogue (Mrs. Horace Hogue) Picture taken by her son shortly before her death in 1953.
–Courtesy of Elizabeth Hogue Vander Pleogh

When we were not having trouble of one kind or another with the peculiar hired help, it was trespassers, neighbors, and tenants. In 1929 my father leased a small portion of the canyon to some people named Reynolds who planned to operate a fish hatchery. They soon struck up a friendship with Dean Hogue, who lived several miles up the canyon at Bixby mountain in the old Bixby ranch house with his mother, Florence Hogue, his wife Vera, and their baby. Dean had been living in Los Angeles where he owned a bakery when the Depression struck, so he had come home. But here he had nothing much to do. His father, a tubercular who had studied for the ministry, was dead, and his mother was a retired school teacher. Dean had little to do beyond chopping wood. (They didn't raise cattle at the Hogue ranch.)

Once or twice a week, Mr. Reynolds had to go to town to buy

fish food—ground liver—and after awhile my parents noticed that whenever he did so, Dean Hogue would come roaring down the canyon in his green pie wagon to visit Mrs. Reynolds and help her feed the fish. They thought nothing of it at first. Mrs. Reynolds was a plain looking woman with washed out blonde hair, pale blue eyes and she wore no make-up; usually she dressed in blue jeans and in her husband's old work shirts; but when she suddenly took to wearing lipstick, mascara, eye shadow and had her hair permanented, they realized that something must be afoot. Dean was the answer, it soon became clear.   In order to reach the fish hatchery, Dean had to come through our gate, and one day he left it open. My father was furious and rushed out to the road, shouting, "Dean, come back and close my gate." Dean paid no attention.

The gate was no more than a chain between two posts over a cattle guard.

But from then on, it became almost a game between the two men although it was played in grim earnest. Every time Dean came down the canyon my father prepared for the confrontation, gun strapped to his hip, but Dean simply stepped on the accelerator and roared down the canyon to the fish hatchery. Soon the two men took to calling each other names, such as "You low-down dirty skunk, you stinking yellow coyote, you pernicious rattlesnake, you cowardly varmint," etc.   This went on for two or three months.   I remember it vividly for it was in the summertime and I was home from school.

One day my father's over-strained patience came to an end. Dean had laughed at him as he roared through the gate. This was too much. Daddy grabbed his gun (this time a high-powered rifle) and started down canyon for the fish hatchery to order Dean off the property. My mother, brother and I were watching anxiously through the back windows of the nursery in the big ranch house. Dean was waiting for my father with a rifle which my father didn't see until he was upon him. Things were very tense for a few minutes with the two men pointing guns at each other. My father was the first to lower his gun. Dean continued to point. Daddy turned and walked back to the house, saying not a word. This was a deep humiliation, having to retreat from his own land, but he knew that if he hadn't one or the other of them would have been dead.

The next day he went to town and purchased a heavy chain and an enormous lock to put on the gate. No one could get through unless my father came out with the key to unlock it. He waited gleefully for Dean. Dean came down in his pie wagon two days later and could not get through. He departed, swearing. My father roared with laughter. But his triumph was not for long. The next day Dean went to town and returned with an enormous pair of metal clippers. He clipped straight through the chain and drove on down to the fish hatchery, laughing as he went.

My father went to Monterey to the D.A.'s office and swore out a complaint. A court date was set for a few weeks later. During the waiting period while Dean continued to come see Mrs. Reynolds behind her husband's back, my father became very nervous. Every night he pulled down all the blinds the minute darkness came; when Mother objected, he said he knew Dean was lurking outside, waiting to take a pot-shot at him. Mother pooh-poohed the idea. She told my father that he was paranoid.

He decided to prove that he was right.

So one night he put his hat on top of the sofa right next to the lighted kerosene lamp in front of a window with the blinds down. Still one could plainly see the hat, silhouetted in the light of the lamp. Around 9 p.m., a bullet came whizzing through the hat.

"You see," Daddy said in triumph.

She saw.

The court case was dismissed by Judge Ray Baugh, who was an old school friend of Dean's. Years later, after Dean Hogue had moved to Kingman, Arizona, my father made a trip to see him and the two men exchanged reminiscences. As it turned out, the reason Dean left the gate open was because he was afraid of my father; he thought that if he got out to close the gate my father, who always carried a gun at his hip, would shoot him. It was a comedy of errors. The whole feud had come about because the two men were afraid of each other—or rather, Dean was afraid and my father enraged in reaction.

They laughed and parted friends.

Flood of 1911 in Mill Creek Canyon. This flood was caused by a log-jam up the creek near the old limekilm.Everyone moved out after this.   —Courtesy of Pat Hathaway

Schooner *Cadensa* at Palo Colorado. Carried tanbark and fence posts. *Nottley's Landing*, 1900.
—Frank Trotter Collection

X.

Sam Trotter, Master Woodsman

When Sam Trotter died in 1937, the very same year the highway opened, the whole Coast mourned, for he had become central to the heart of this far-flung Down Coast community, loved by all.

S am Trotter, one of the most beloved characters on the Coast, lived at the mouth of Palo Colorado Canyon three miles north of us in a house built by I.N. Swetnam in the 1890s. A beautiful house of hand-hewn redwood logs, it is painted red, caulked with white, and stands there today, one of the two remaining testaments to the past. (The other is the old Post ranch house built in 1877, which stands next to the Ventana restaurant at Big Sur and is also painted red.)

Sam Trotter lived in the tall, narrow house at Palo Colorado from 1906 until 1923 after his marriage to Adelaide Pfeiffer, and there their five children were born: Roy, Henry, Lillian, Frank and Walter. Of these only two remained on the Coast to become an integral part of its life. Frank and Walter carried on in their father's tradition as woodsmen, house builders, road builders and helpers of their neighbors in all emergencies. Frank and Walter still live in the Big Sur today but have retired.

It has often been said, especially down in the Big Sur where Sam finally settled, that without the Trotters it is hard to see how most of the settlers survived, especially after the colony at Coastlands—the Coastlands Association—was built in the 1920s. These were "city folk." Sam built the log house or Trails Club, now part of the restaurant Nepenthe, as well as most of the houses and roads there. He also built on Partington Ridge. When Sam Trotter died in 1937, the very same year the highway opened, the whole Coast mourned, for he had become central to the heart of this far-flung Down Coast community, loved by all.

In retrospect it seems strangely symbolic that his death, like that of a giant redwood tree or ancient oak falling in the forest, should have coincided with the ending of its isolation and of its colorful pioneer history—the beginning of a new, less romantic and less exciting modern era. Nothing was ever to be the same again.

Interesting newcomers came in, but nothing was as it had been in "the old days." It couldn't be.

Sam Trotter was born in Missouri in 1871 and came to California in 1891 at the age of 20 because he had gotten himself in trouble by getting engaged to two girls at once, Molly and Susie. He was already engaged to Molly when he fell in love with Susie; the situation was too much for him, so he left.

For a time he worked at Boulder Creek for Bill and George Nottley in the lumber industry. Then, in 1893, the Nottley's got a letter from I.N. Swetnam who lived at

Sam Trotter, the Missourian who came west because he got engaged to two girls at once and couldn't decide between them. He ended up as the Coast's most beloved and depended upon character.
—Collection of Frank Trotter

Garapata Creek, telling them there was good timber land in the north fork of Little River (Little Sur). They decided to go down and investigate.

Old Coast Road at Palo Colorado
—Collection of Frank Trotter

Sam Trotter kept a journal of his first visit to the wild Monterey Coast. it took them all day to get from Carmel and the Hatton ranch and dairy, making various stops and visits at Carmel Highlands, to the Garapata where

The Trotter house at Palo Colorado where they lived from 1906 until 1923. All five children were born here. Originally the house was built by I.N. Swetnam, and Sam Trotter sold it to Corbett Grimes.
— Collection of Frank Trotter

they stayed overnight with Swetnam, then proceeded on their journey to the Little Sur via Palo Colorado Canyon where they stopped at the Starretts and the Murrays.

"Mrs. Murray was one of the finest little ladies I had ever met and talked to," wrote Sam. "She and her husband had lived there since 1875. He had died and she and her two sons Robert and Ned, and her daughter, Eugenia, had carried on the ranch, raising cattle and horses."

It was this same Ned Murray, son of Mrs. Murray, who got

involved with the ill-fated Cushing girl and took off for China, never to be heard of again. His brother Robert and his sister Eugenia, who became a school teacher, stayed on at the ranch.

Coastlands, with the Trails Club (log cabin built by Sam Trotter) standing. This later became Nepenthe. — Collection of Frank Trotter

After several days camping out in the Little Sur and exploring the terrain, the Nottleys and Sam Trotter returned to Boulder

Creek where Trotter re-
mained until 1894.

"I left Boulder Creek all of a
sudden," he wrote in his
journal. "After I left I was
accused of something I did
not do and later the party
concerned put out a notice in
the paper stating it was a false
report which made me feel
better."

Log House at Trails Club, 1920s.
—Collection of Frank Trotter

With his partner Louie York, Sam took off for his cabin in
Little River (Little Sur). On their way to Little River, they
went through Mill Creek, for they had learned there was a
road up Mill Creek to the Bixby ranch.

"So we drove up to the Bixby ranch which was a steep road but
before we got to the ranch house we discovered Bixby had a
very fine ranch. After we got out of the redwood and oak timber we found hay field and pastured land. Mr. Bixby proved to
be a fine man and later a good neighbor. He and his wife lived
there with one son, George Bixby, and daughter, Alta.

"The ranch contained something over a thousand acres. He
owned 100 to 125 head of cattle, quite a bunch of hogs, had
seven saddle horses and work stock, and raised considerable
hay and barley to fatten his hogs. On his ranch he had
considerable redwood timber and tan oak."

From there Sam and Louie proceeded to Little River where
they build a cabin on Sam's claim. Louie had malaria.

"As Louie helped me most of the time I was watching him
and his chills and he hadn't had a chill for several days. I
asked him when he had his last chill and he had to think and

he had forgotten when it was the fever had left him. Fresh air, sweet water from the redwood gulch and lime formation, fresh beef, trout, quail—and chills and fever had no chance where one takes plenty of exercise."

Old Coast road. Wagon loaded with tanbark headed for Nottley's Landing.
—Collection of Frank Trotter

After five or six weeks in Little River, they made a trip out for supplies. After stopping at Mill Creek where a man named McCullum was running the Sur post office, then at the Smith ranch at Rocky Creek and at Nottley's in the Garapata where Nottley had a camp and was commencing lumber operations, they decided to change their plans and explore the country farther south down the Coast.

They went back to the Bixby ranch where Sam borrowed a horse.

"On top of Serra Hill," he wrote, "is a low gap in the ridge. We went down a 12 to 15% grade. To the right we had a fine view of the ocean, about five miles out, and Pico Blanco mountain, south fork of Little River and a part of the old Cooper land grant. By this time, we were on the Cunningham ranch. Off to the right was their home. High up was the Jack Howland ranch and still higher up over the ocean the Heath ranch. A widow woman and her daughter, Serena Heath... Mrs. Heath was nick-named Leather Britches."

From here, Sam passed the Gschwend place (it was Gschwend who had leveled Little Sur grade in 1881 with a handmade level), the Romer place, the José de la Torre blacksmith shop, the Cooper ranch, the Molera ranch and the Pfeiffer ranch.

By this time they were far down into the Big Sur, a country very different from the northern section of the Coast, being brighter, sunnier, with huge sprawling, grass-covered hills but no wide-mouthed canyons permitting easy access to the sea.

The old Coast road at Palo Colorado, going north, as seen from the Trotter House (originally the Swetnam house) at the mouth of the canyon.

—Collection of Frank Trotter

There were beaches, but one could only reach them by climbing down perpendicular cliffs. (Except at Sycamore Canyon.)

"From Post's ranch," he continued, "We left the divide and took the trail. No road from Post's down as far as San

Simeon, which was 100 miles by trail and damn poor trail at that.... On leaving Post's ranch the trail ran along the side of the mountain overlooking the ocean and about 500 hundred feet above sea level."

The three men (Sam Trotter, Louie York and Bill Nottley who had accompanied them on this trip of exploration) continued on their way to Partington Ridge, stopping at every ranch house along the way, including the Castros, the Ed Grimes (Mrs. Grimes was the former Ellen Post), Harry Laffler, and de la Torre. (Mrs. de la Torre had been Mary Post.)

Nottley's Landing in 1900. One of the most important landings on the Coast. (Others were Bixby, Anderson and Partington.) At mouth of Palo Colorado Canyon. —Collection of Frank Trotter

Along with Bill Nottley, Sam explored the tanbark possibilities of Partington Ridge, but they decided it was better in Garapata and the Palo Colorado, for that was where Nottley established his boat landing the following year.

Later, Nottley's Landing was to become famous for its dance hall where gatherings took place every Saturday night with guitar and fiddle music; often these were raucous and violent affairs.

One his way back, Sam Trotter attended a dance at Cooper Hall after stopping at the Castro ranch for lunch. The account from his journal is given in detail as it affords us a vivid picture of life at the time.

"They told me that they were all going to the dance in a wagon and would start early to get there before dark and I could go with them in the wagon and get your horse tomorrow when we got back. I was ready to accept their invitation when I remembered that I had told Miss Bixby I would try to get to the dance and remembering about Mollie and Susie I did not want any complications and trouble."

There were three Castro girls, sisters of Roche Castro, whose mother was cousin to the famous bandit Tiburcio Vasquez. They had been singing songs accompanied by a guitar.

"I appeared to like Lorena the best," Sam wrote. "They told me that the dance was going to be a Cascarone dance. A cascarone is an empty egg shell stuffed with confetti. A gentleman breaks a cascarone over a lady's head. The confetti falls down on the lady's shoulders which as I understand explains to others who see it that she is his favorite lady and choice for the evening. And she will do the same thing; the first man she breaks a shell over is her favored partner for the evening. It may be the man that broke a cascarone over her head or it may be someone else."

This was an old Spanish custom that had reached California and the Sur from Mexico.

After lunch (actually the main meal of the day), Trotter started for the dance hall up the Coast at Big Sur.

"I was surprised to see several horses and wagons already there, and they had men taking care of the horses as they came in, directing them in certain places for the night... I seen George and Alta Bixby ride in. They went direct to the hay rack where my horse was tied; they recognized their own horse which I was riding. I saw they looked over the others horses and failed to see that their father's and Nottley's horses had arrived. So I knew they were reading signs. I walked over to meet them.

"I told them I had deserted their father and Nottley and had arrived just ahead of them. They said they had figured that much out. George Bixby and I walked over to the barbecue pit; Alta went to the house. They were burning down, getting it ready to cook or barbecue the beef. I saw a large beef they were cutting up to have for supper.

"The crowd had all arrived by dark except a few horseback riders came in later. I was surprised to see so many gathered together in one place, where one would think so few people lived, but there, I am certain was more than a hundred people. The music had arrived, an accordion player, guitar and banjo. Immediately after dark the lamps were lighted and the music began and a few couples started dancing. Most of the crowd was waiting for the barbecued meat. I was undecided which girl to ask for a dance first, Miss Bixby or Miss Lorena Castro, until it was settled for me by chance when someone came by and taken the Castro girl and started dancing, then I asked Alta for a dance just as another man came after her but I spoke first which was my start in the Big Sur country. From then on until the next morning we had a few dances, then we were told the barbecued beef was ready for the first call.

"Mrs. Castro had asked me to eat with them as they had extra food such as pie, cake, tomatoes, fried chicken.... The beef was barbecued by experts and was wonderful with plenty of sauce and French bread. Baked beans, also Spanish boiled beans, with plenty of chili peppers but not too much for most people, plenty of good strong coffee... I managed to strain my stomach almost to the breaking point."

(All of the Trotter men were noted for their enormous capacity for food, on which hangs many a tale told to this day down in Big Sur.)

Sam Trotter and his first wife, Abigail Gregg (sister of Charlie Gregg). She died tragically young of tuberculosis.
— Collection of Frank Trotter

Adelaide Pfeiffer, Sam's second wife and the mother of his five children. They lived at Palo Colorado from 1906-1923.
— Collection of Frank Trotter

This was Sam Trotter's introduction to the social life of the Big Sur in the late 1890s at it best. Still in the Spanish tradition, it followed the ways instituted at the Cooper ranch at El Sur. Sam liked it and its people so well that he decided to remain there. He first married Abigail Gregg, the sister of Charlie Gregg who married Alta Bixby. But Abby, this lovely young woman with whom he was deeply in love, was fatally ill of tuberculosis and died at the age of 26. He told my mother that he continued to love Abby all his life. Every day he carried her in his arms to watch the sunset.

Then after a period of deep mourning, he married the handsome Adelaide Pfeiffer, one of the eight Pfeiffer children. It was with Adelaide that he settled at Palo Colorado, buying the Swetnam house in 1906, where they had five children.

Walter and Frank Trotter in the tubs at Hot Springs in 1940—originally Slate's Spring. There were only two tubs. One put up a flag to show occupancy. Today this is the exclusive and esoteric Esalen Institute.   —Collection of Frank Trotter

Handsome as Adelaide Pfeiffer Trotter was, she unfortunately—from Sam Trotter's standpoint—was more drawn to ranch and outdoor life than she was to domestic life and things about the house. Whenever he gave her money for curtains or for a new dress, she'd spend it on livestock or fencing. One day, as he told my mother years later, he could stand it no longer and took off, faking a suicide in order to do it.

My father was the one who found Sam Trotter's wallet and bandana and the wheelmarks of a car going off the road at Carmel Highlands one day on his way home from town. He sent for the Sheriff. The conclusion was that Sam Trotter had driven over the cliff and killed himself.

In reality, Sam had gone north and gotten himself a job in the lumber industry.

It was a considerable length of time before word came to Adelaide that Sam was yet alive. She was so deeply distressed and heartbroken by his desertion that she had a nervous breakdown and died shortly thereafter. When word reached Sam of this, he rushed home to taken care of his children.

I remember one day Sam Trotter stopped by our place at Mill Creek with a big wagonload of apples which he had evidently gotten farther down the Coast, most probably from the Post's who had a big apple orchard. Trotter had some German blood in his background and it lingered in his accent. He said to my mother, "I got these *apfels* because I think *apfels* are good for children. Don't you think they are good for children?"

Mother agreed that they were. Sam never married again and it was Lillian, the only girl in the family, who did the housework and took care of her brothers in the years of her growing up. "She worked like a slave," Mother said. As I remember, she was an attractive girl, about six years older than I was.

Frank Trotter and I, born the same year, went to high school together, and he and his wife Fern, who has a distinct musical talent, still remain my good friends. Younger brother, Walter, unfortunately has emphysema. Both live in the Big Sur.

Top row left: Caterpillar man—"Dutch Bowles", Douglas Mellville, Gui (Jaime's daughter), Jaime de Angulo. Bottom row left: Sam Trotter, Pearl Smith, unknown.

—Collection of Sam Trotter

XI.

Jaime de Angulo's Notorious Feud with Boronda

Jaime de Angulo came riding down our hill to Rainbow Lodge on a black stallion, wearing black chaps, a black shirt and a black sombrero, along with a huge turquoise-studded Indian silver conche belt from New Mexico. His long black hair flowing in the wind, his blue eyes flashing, he was beautiful rather than handsome and was given to passionate gestures, speaking with his hands as well as his tongue.

O f the many feuds that occurred on the Coast, the most colorful was the feud between the eminent but eccentric Dr. Jaime de Angulo and Alejandrino Borondo in a dispute over cattle. Its real origins, however, went back to an earlier period when de Angulo, Boronda and Roche Castro were wheeling up and down the Coast on horseback, getting drunk together and playing the part of gay caballeros. My mother believed they supplied most of the local color found in Ruth Comfort Mitchell's novel *Corduroy Road*, published in 1915. Tourists coming to Pfeiffer's Resort, which had started up in business in 1910, thought the country was full of bandits and Spanish dons due to the appearance of the picturesque trio; moreover they heard tales, largely fictional, of the bandits and outcasts who lived farther south beyond the reach of the wagon road.

Jaime de Angulo was a medical doctor turned anthropologist who had bought a ranch at Big Sur in 1914 from Roche Castro. His appearance, in the 1920s when I first saw him, was dramatic in the extreme. He came riding down our hill to Rainbow Lodge on a black stallion, wearing black chaps, a black shirt and a black sombrero, along with a huge turquoise-studded Indian silver conche belt from New Mexico. His long black hair flowing in the wind, his blue eyes flashing, he was beautiful rather than handsome and was given to passionate gestures, speaking with his hands as well as his tongue. And he talked rapidly, brilliantly, usually about linguistics, the American Indians, or Freud. He tried to make love to my mother and called her a bourgeois when she refused.

Born in Paris in 1887, the son of a Spanish nobleman who had fled Madrid for political reasons, Jaime had attended two Jesuit schools in Paris and was expelled from both of them for not having a cooperative spirit in religion. Later Jaime became an atheist. He was interested in science, chiefly physics and chemistry, but these studies were not permitted by the Jesuits. At the age of 18, after a violent quarrel with his father, he fled to America where he worked as a cowboy on a western ranch, then as an overseer of a convict labor camp in Honduras. He landed in San Francisco in 1906 just at the time of the earthquake and escaped to Santa Maria where he took refuge in a whorehouse as the guest of the Madame.

"I never sobered up until I left," he told me at his ranch on Partington Ridge years later. He was just 19 but had already started to drink heavily, a problem which was to plague him off and on throughout his life.

In 1907 he went to Johns Hopkins where he got a degree in medicine and married a fellow student, Cary Fink of Virginia. Both believed in eugenic marriage. Neither of them wanted to go into medical practice. As Jaime put it, "It was not considered elegant at the time."

Jaime's special field was genetics and on this account he went to Stanford to do research on the fruit-fly. But on a trip to Northern California he bought a horse ranch at Alturas and ended up studying the Pit River Indians whose territory this was. He learned how to record their language, and became fascinated with the entire field of linguistics. He ended up recording the extraordinary total of 27 Indian languages. Most of his field work was done in northern California with Pit River, Modoc and other tribes, but he also worked in Mexico and in the American southwest, mainly New Mexico where he was a guest of Mabel Dodge Luhan and her Taos Indian husband, Tony. His article on his early experiences at Pit River was published in the Hudson Review under the title "Indians in Overalls."

Cary de Angulo accompanied Jaime on many of his field trips but she also worked independently. One time in Carmel, where he had built a log house, he got a telegram from Cary who was up at Alturas.

Dr. Jaime de Angulo, long hair and all, in his younger years at Partington Ridge, with Dutch, the Caterpillar operator. Note unique headband.   —Collection of Frank Trotter

"Send condoms. Doing research with the chief."

"And did you?" I asked.

"I did."

Jaime's daughter, Gui de Angulo, says this never happened. "Jaime was an awful liar," she commented.

It is said that Jaime, galloping along the beach on his Arab stallion, was one of Carmel's more picturesque figures and that in 1914, shortly after the Jeffers moved to Carmel, they met near Carmel Point. Jaime asked them to dinner. They were very hungry, and as they sat watching him cook a marvelous steak they could hardly wait; then Jaime gave the steak to his dog.

Improbable as this may seem, those who knew swore it was true and the Jeffers went home hungry to their log cabin on Monteverde Street, and scrounged up some leftovers.

Cary de Angulo's principal interest was not in anthropology and linguistics, but in psychology, however, and later, as Cary Baynes (after divorcing Jaime) she became Carl Jung's translator. Jaime, too, was interested in psychology, for, following World War I in which he had served as a medical doctor dealing with shell-shock victims, the Army sent him to school in Europe to study psychiatry. It was here that he worked with Freud and was one of the first to introduce his theories to America. His daughter by his first marriage was named Ximena after the wife of the Cid, and still lives in Switzerland.

His second wife was Nancy Freeland, a writer, by whom he had two children, Alvar and Ysabel Guiomar.

He was living in Carmel in 1914, in between making field trips to northern California, when he first learned of the existence of the Big Sur.

"I saw Antonio and Roche Castro in Carmel wearing chaps," he related. " I asked them if there was any land for sale down the coast. I asked them where they came from. They said, 'To hell and gone.' Antonio suggested Roche sell me his homestead on Partington Ridge. 'You can't make a living there,' they told me. Next week I came down the Coast. I met Boronda, who was a cousin of Castro's, and he had leased his home ranch from an old lady. I cried, 'This is the country where I want to live; and this is what I have been looking for.'"

Jaime bought Roche's homestead for ten dollars an acre, one half down and one half when he had proved up on the homestead. It took five years to prove up on a homestead.

"I asked Roche Castro to stay for awhile, because I was a greenhorn, and I wanted Roche to show me how to run cattle, etc., until the end of the year."

According to Jaime, Roche's father, David Castro, was the best roper in California. "He never missed, not once, and could rope from any position, not looking. He used a 20 foot loop."

Jaime and Roche along with Boronda spoke Spanish and got drunk together, and, riding up and down the Coast trail on horseback, gave outsiders the impression that the days of the dons had not yet ended.

All was well until Jaime and Roche persuaded Borondo to marry a woman Roche had recently jilted. Her name was Grace and she lived in Berkeley. They had met, liked each other, but just before she was due to arrive for the wedding Roche met a woman with a brutal husband and three children with whom he fell deeply and instantly in love. He rescued her from her husband and wrote Grace to break things off.

One night Roche and Jaime stopped in at Boronda's place and, as usual, got drunk on red wine. Very drunk.

"Let's marry the old buzzard to the woman you jilted," Jaime said to Roche. Boronda appeared to like the idea.

"I'll save some money and quit drinking," he said.

Then he began to have doubts.

"I'm lame," he protested.

"A lame man in bed is just as good as a two legged man," said Jaime.

"I can't write," he said.

"I can," said Jaime.

Jaime and Roche put their heads together and composed a

letter in Alejandrino Boronda's name, proposing marriage. The woman accepted and came down to Big Sur on the mail stage. When she later discovered that Roche and Jaime together had actually framed the letter and that it was Jaime's handwriting, she was justifiably furious. She told her husband's two friends that they were unwelcome at the ranch and never to come there or even to speak to them again.

Grace Boronda, according to Florence Hogue, was quite an unusual person herself. "She was a wild bird among the tame ones," she said. She was not only a diginified but a singularly imaginative and sensitive person. She was certainly not conventional or she would not have consented to marry, in the wild Big Sur hills, a man she nad never met.

But it is not to be wondered at that she was furious with Roche, her ex-fiance, and Jaime.

Boronda quit drinking.

"After that Boronda began not to see people," Jaime related. "He grew sour. He got into a feud with Roche, his cousin, and accused him of being a murderer and an outlaw. This was untrue. The real trouble was over mules. But Boronda wanted to run Roche out of the country."

Since Jaime remained Roche's friend, Boronda hated him, too.

Boronda made war on Jaime in the early 1930s by letting his cattle trespass on Jaime's land. This infuriated Jaime who was raising horses as well as cattle. Again and again he warned Boronda to keep his cattle off his ranch but Boronda paid no attention.

It was at this very same time that Jaime decided to have a dude ranch at his place—Rancho Los Pesares, or the Ranch of the Sorrows. The year was 1932 and my father had just completed his Stone House at the northern end of Bixby Creek Bridge (then called Rainbow Bridge) which was under construction at the time. The Depression had hit America. It had not too seriously hit Jaime since his wife had some money, but all the same they did not have as much to live on as they had had before.

The dude ranch that Jaime dreamed up was undoubtedly the most bizarre that had ever come into existence. Jaime wrote the prospectus, and his wife, Nancy Freeland (a professional writer) and his partner in the venture, a woman named Jewel, both approved of it and thought it would make the dude ranch a great success.

The prospectus, read as follows:

EL RANCHITO LOS PESARES, BIG SUR.
Monterey County, California

This would like to be a dude ranch, but it isn't. In fact, it's very hard to describe this place because it does not resemble anything else. If you are looking for crooning cowboys, don't come here! Not a cowboy on the place, not a cow, not even a picturesque corral.

If you are looking for comfort, don't come here! You will have to sleep in a tent or under the stars. This place is still in the wilderness, far from civilization.

The food is nothing extra. The cook is crazy. Sometimes he cooks in Chinese, sometimes in French, and again in Spanish, and sometimes in his own. He cooks when he pleases but he never objects to your using his pots and pans nor his kitchen. Anyway, the kitchen is also the dining room, and the dining room is also the living room, and there is nothing cozy about any of them.

If you expect good horses, don't come here! The
country is too rough for good horses. You cannot
trot, much less gallop anywhere around here. Our
horses are as sure-footed as goats (otherwise they
would not have survived) but even at a walk you
risk your neck at every turn of the trail—and the
risk is yours.

If you expect good fishing, do not come here! The
streams back in the hills are full of SMALL trout
that is not sport. But to get there....! It takes a whole
day's riding to get there over an abominable trail.
In fact, it's not a real trail... nobody goes there.

We will take you there any time you like, and
cheerfully. We are used to it—but you aren't.
Saddle-weary and tired, you will have to sleep on
the ground in a weird canyon. You won't be able to
sleep. You will get the heebie-jeebies, and you'll
spend the night feeding the fire.

The caballerango-guide is as crazy as the cook, and
furthermore he is bad tempered. His language is
awful. So, if you are squeamish, bring some cotton
for your ears.

We have warned you candidly of the lack of
comfort in this primitive place. But if you care to
risk coming, then bring the roughest kinds of
clothes, a bathing suit (the beach is right under us,
but 1600 feet below), your rifle (ours is not very
good); besides deer you will find here quail—both
valley and mountain—wild pigeons, doves,
squirrels, pumas, lynxes, foxes, coyotes and coons.
Bring your own tackle (surf and stream). We're not
sportsmen. We catch them in our hats.

Bring your own literature. You will find nothing
here except a collection of *New Yorkers* and
National Geographics, several books on botany, a
few silly novels and a couple of scientific works.

As to the weather, in April and even May it is still
pretty raw, but the hills are at their greenest, and the

wild flowers in bloom. In June we are liable to shiver
in the fog a whole week, and the hills are beginning
to turn yellow. July and August are fairly good,
sometimes hot. But from then on to Christmas it is
wonderful! Lazy, soft days full of languor and
longing, the ocean so still, the hills asleep in the
warm sunshine. From Christmas till April it is hell,
with one storm on the heels of the last.

In very tiny print Jaime ended with the following:

Our rates are ten dollars a day, flat. This includes
everything: food, horses, camping trips, guides, and
everything!   Children ought to pay double, but if
they are handsome and intelligent they pay just like
the others.

Our address: Los Pesares, Big Sur, California. (For
telegrams, add 'Mail from Monterey'). We cannot
care for more than six.

"And remember, dearie, no recriminations."

This brilliant literary effort attracted no interest and nobody
turned up at Ranchitos Los Pesares. Not one single tourist
appeared during the long hot summer on Partington Ridge.
Jaime's partner, Jewel, became restless. She had expected to
make a lot of money and was frustrated that there was none.

It was just at this juncture that Jaime's feud with Boronda
reached a flaming height. Jaime got so angry that he began
shooting Boronda's cattle.

"First I shot a cow," Jaime told me. "I gave a part to everyone
on the Coast, as I wanted him to hear of it. Then, two weeks
later, I shot five altogether. I wanted Boronda to know of it so
Boronda would end his trespassing. Since the dude ranch was a
failure, Jewel wanted to leave and Nancy gave her $200 so that
she could present no claim.   But Jewel, after leaving my

ranch on Partington Ridge, drove straight to the D.A.'s office."

She turned Jaime in for cattle rustling. The next day the Deputy D.A., and a man from the Cattleman's Association came down to the Big Sur on horseback with a warrant for Jaime's arrest. Jewel had been keeping a diary. In her diary she noted down the exact locations of the bones of the cattle Jaime had shot.

"'Here's her diary,' they said, and they got Mustang Pete, who was working for me, to take them to the bones. They threatened to take him to San Quentin if he didn't tell on me. Mustang Pete was a horse-breaker. So Mustang Pete led them to the bones."

According to the warrant, Dr. Jaime de Angulo was charged with "violating health laws, for slaughtering cattle without a permit."

In the car, the Deputy Sheriff said to Jaime, "Don't tell me anything. I don't want to hear it."

As Jaime discovered later, they thought he belonged to a gang of cattle rustlers they had been watching. Jewel had told the authorities a lurid tale and received a reward of $500.

They took Jaime to Salinas to the County jail.

"I couldn't get bail. It was too late," he told me. "But they didn't put me in the bullpen. They put me in the women's cell. There weren't any women there at the time. 'You can't smoke here,' they told me, 'but call me when you want to.' They locked me in. I had claustrophobia. I began to shriek. I had hysterics. 'Open, open, I am going insane.' I shouted. I had a real case of claustrophobia. 'I thought I could stand it but I can't. I'm going insane,' I told them."

When they discovered Dr. de Angulo was a medical doctor they took him seriously. The Sheriff was summoned. They took Jaime to the Kimball Hotel in Monterey where he was given an entire suite at the expense of the County until he was arraigned.

When the case came to trial, Jaime was put on probation. The Judge wanted to let him off entirely but could not on account of a technicality. Ordinarily, on probation, he would have been confined to Monterey County, but the Judge bent the rules. "You may have wine and the freedom of the State instead of the County," he told him.

The story was written up in a sensational manner by the *New York Times,* the *New Republic,* the *Nation,* the *Literary Digest* and various international publications. "Noted Anthropologist Acquitted from Grand Larceny Charge on Plea of Claustrophobia," one headline read.

The original charge of cattle rustling had been changed to grand larcency in order to make probation possible.

Jaime, who ordinarily knew no shame, was oddly embarrassed about this incident, for, as he explained to me, in his family it was a disgrace to have one's name in the papers except when one was born, when one married, or when one died. But later on he made the papers again.

"I was found making political speeches to the moon, to ghosts," he said. "But I was given only a $10 fine and was bailed out of jail."

The last time I saw Dr. Jaime de Angulo he was riding a mule and leading another mule, the latter weighted down with baskets of stones. He had a black patch over one eye and was wearing a green eye-shade; otherwise he was stark naked except for a filthy pair of jeans and a wicked looking knife stuck in his belt. The belt I vaguely recognized as a woven Navajo belt I had given him some years earlier which was red and white; but now it was black, its pattern indistinguishable.

Gone was the romantic figure of my childhood. He looked rather like a Spanish brigand and the scene might easily have been the Pyrenees, but was actually down at his ranch, Rancho Los Pesares, the Ranch of the Sorrows. And indeed it had become that since his six year old son Alvar had been killed in a motor accident and was buried there. Here Jaime lived until shortly before his death in 1950. This eccentric genius who had been at one time an internationally noted anthropologist spent the latter part of his life in obscurity, forgotten even by his colleagues. Ironically enough it was not until after his death that his work was recognized with the publication of his classic *Indian Tales* about Coyote Old Man, which he had originally written (and illustrated) for his children.

"Why the stones?" I asked him in amazement that day.

"Hell, I'm pack-breaking her," he cried. "Darling, it's good to see you, and you've got your stockings on straight for once. Who's the man with you?   Are you sleeping with him? Come on down to the house and we'll have some red wine."

He had spotted the half gallon of red wine I was carrying under my right arm as I never went to visit Jaime without bringing wine.

Jaime was unquestionably one of the most brilliant men I ever met and the most eccentric. There was a feeling, especially when he talked of anthropology, linguistics, mathematics, physics, psychiatry, philosophy, fields he knew well, of extraordinary lucidity—rather like a pure gem in whose center existed a deep, still, quiet pool, rather like a crystal. The feeling one got at such moments was of pure beauty; and it was at times such as these that those who knew Jaime felt to the fullest the purity of his genius which, when so directly contacted, was akin to music, poetry, the stars, flame, the cosmos.

But Jaime had also a dark side, a perverse and contradictory side—and his enemies called him crazy, bohemian, drunken, dangerous, even a devil. Although he denied it, his temperament was very Spanish. His dramatic sense, his need to play a role, to be a buffoon, a star, a madman, a tragic figure, a rebel, a martyr, ruled his life and made it in the end a wasteland, a tragedy—except for his work which was unquestionably the work of a genius. Jaime professed to hate Spaniards and the Spanish temperament. This he had gotten from his father, a Spanish nobleman, who thought all Spaniards were barbarians. Jaime once stated to me categorically that all Spaniards were "brutish, insolent, haughty, impolite and boorish"—adjectives which could at times have been applied to himself.

He no longer had a car in those last years at the ranch. He had had too many wrecks, including the one in which his only son was killed. Once he carelessly threw a lighted match on top of a can of kerosene in back of the car and burned up his manuscript on the Chinese language, said to be the best of its kind in the world. He re-wrote the entire book, but evidently it got lost as it never turned up among his papers. Jaime rode horseback when he went anywhere, but there was one stallion he gave up riding permanently owing to the fact that he had ridden him down to the highway from his ranch on Partington Ridge in only ten minutes. Jaime was drunk; it could have killed the stallion. He put him out to pasture after that.

Van Wyck Brooks described him in *Scenes of Portraits* a bit unfairly but picturesquely:

> *In Carmel I spent several months before the college*
> *term began...living in the al fresco fashion that*

everybody practices in this quite romantic peninsula of Monterey. The wild past was still present there with even the remains of an outlaw's camp, the hut of Joaquin Murietta in San Jose Canyon, where Easter lilies grew as daisies do elsewhere, and there was the forest scenery that Robert Louis Stevenson, after his visit, pictured in Treasure Island. There were the whitewashed Mexican shanties of John Steinbeck's Tortilla Flat and the old adobe house where John Steinbeck was living when I returned to the Peninsula later. If, moreover, one no longer saw the caballeros of the eighteen-forties with strings of bells on their embroidered pantaloons, Jaime de Angulo, with his Arab horse and his red sash and El Greco beard, had all the look of a remnant from the earlier time. This was the Spanish ethnologist-doctor who had lived with the Indians in the southwest, where he collected the Indian tales that he was to put into final form as a dying man forty years later on his mountain top ranch. There was never a figure more fantastic than Jaime de Angulo came to be in those days; when, living alone looking out at the Pacific, a decayed Don Quixote, ragged and mad, he boxed with a pet stallion and carved his meat with a great knife that hung from his middle.

Henry Miller also described Jaime in his book, *A Devil in Paradise,* and said that there was "something satanic about him." Jaime often turned up at Henry's house on Partington Ridge, a few miles down the road from his ranch, and ended up insulting and abusing everyone. Invariably Henry had given him something to drink, and Jaime was very sensitive to alcohol.

Jaime could be gay and brilliant when drinking (he always was when I was there) and would dance and sing Indian chants he had collected in the Southwest, sounding sometimes like a coyote howling at the moon. His favorite Indians, however, were the Pit River tribe whom he had first gotten to know after he bought the Alturas ranch in 1913. Even as an old man, bearded and grizzled with a black patch over one eye, without that spectacular beauty which as a young man had made him a romantic figure, he had a beauty that outshone his age and raggedness.

He looked rather like an El Greco Christ, although I am sure no one would have called him Christ-like.

Jaime's daughter, Gui, has recently published a book on her father entitled *Jaime in Taos* and is soon coming forth with a complete biographical portrait of him.

No doubt, when this happens, his monographs on Indian languages will be dug out of the anthropological files and translated into English. (In a fit of pique, due to a falling out with his colleagues, he wrote them all in French, believing that they could not read French. The gesture boomeranged, of course.)

His colleagues at the University of California, although they liked him personally—men such as Kroeber, Sapir, Lowe—disapproved of his way of doing field work. This was an era in which respectable ethnologists sedately went forth, notebook and record player in hand; but instead of this, Jaime got drunk with shamen and rolled in ditches with them. In this way he got to know them as no one else could or would.

Nevertheless, he taught some courses at the University one summer, but due to his eccentric behavior the authorities did not rehire him.

It was during this period, when he was living with Nancy in Berkeley, that he became interested in discovering what it felt like to be a woman. He let his hair grow long, even longer than it had been, and went about in women's clothing. Nancy schooled him in how to stand, walk and sit. The one thing that betrayed him was his voice.   One day, when first practicing in "drag," he and Nancy stopped at a grocery store and Jaime got worried for fear Nancy was going to forget the avocados. Finally he could stand it no longer and squawked out "Avocados" in a high falsetto voice. Everyone turned and stared. Jaime never opened his mouth when in "drag" after that.

His long hair inevitably aroused comment on the campus and it soon became bruited about that Dr. de Angulo was going over to San Francisco on the ferry, dressed as a woman, picking up men on Market Street. This, however, the campus authorities were willing to overlook; but one day Jaime got drunk and climbed the flag pole naked. On this same morning he had turned up at an 8 o'clock class dressed in tuxedo and white tie.

This ended his University career—or so he told me years later at the ranch.

After that, he devoted his time to working with the Indians, recording their languages and dividing his time between the Alturas ranch and Big Sur. (But he finally sold Alturas and moved to Big Sur permanently.)

After Nancy and his daughter, Guiomar (now Gui) left the ranch in 1938 so that Gui could attend school in Berkeley (formerly her father had taught her at the ranch) Jaime grew increasingly slovenly. His house was filled with beds which were concrete slabs on top of which mattresses and bedding were placed, sometimes only bedding. There were numerous fireplaces, built like New Mexico fireplaces, some bee hive shaped with antlers above them. All the bedrooms let off onto an outside terrace, no corridor between. The roof looked like a patch work quilt, it had been mended so often, and in different colors—such as orange, green, red, yellow. In the living room, if you could call it that since it was not detached from the rest of the house, he had a wood stove, and on this he did his cooking. It was a small ordinary wood stove, the kind that is used for heating, not for cooking; and it had no stove pipe. There was a smoke hole in the ceiling, like an Indian smoke-hole, but when the wind wasn't blowing right the room got very filled with smoke. Guests simply had to put up with it.

After Nancy and Gui's departure, Jaime lived in filth. There is no other word for it. His clothes were dirty; his blue jeans could have stood up by themselves; and his dishes were dirty. He thought hygiene a lot of nonsense despite his medical training. He had found, in the course of living with the Indians, that such things mattered less than people thought they did.

He washed dishes in cold water without soap. Every plate, cup or glass was encrusted with dirt or grease and one simply had to ignore it. It was really difficult to drink out of a filthy glass that looked as if it hadn't been washed for decades, but grimly one somehow managed—wearing a smile on one's face.

One day I arrived at Jaime's at lunch time, having walked up the steep trail from the highway, and he invited me to lunch. We ate stewed chicken, sitting out at the long refectory table overlooking the ocean, and we talked about anthropology, marriage and marriage customs in various primitive societies. Jaime disapproved of marriage and advocated free love—except for eugenic marriage. Marriage, except when it led to the production of children, confined the spirit and destroyed relationships, he emphasized. He was very impassioned on this subject so I kept quiet.

The stewed chicken was very good considering the fact that it had not been thoroughly cleaned and still had some feathers on it and that underneath the table the entrails were being devoured by hornets. I ignored all this. I am sure Jaime

Dr. Jaime de Angulo, in elegant attire, delivering his weekly broadcast at KPFA, Berkeley. This was shortly before his death of cancer. His book, *Indian Tales*, was published in 1953. A classic.
—Collection of author

would have been amused if he had known what I was thinking. "Well, so you wanted to be an anthropologist. You wanted to do field work and live among primitive peoples. If I were one I would have to eat locusts, grasshoppers, worms, the entrails of cows, cow's eyes, dogs and rotten fish. I am very lucky to be eating this partially cleaned chicken and that my one and only field trip is at the home of an anthropologist."

After my marriage to Pat Wall in 1948 I went to Mexico and lost touch with Jaime. When I returned to California the following spring I learned that he had left the ranch because he had cancer and had moved to Berkeley. In Berkeley he did a regular radio program on KPFA called "Indian Tales." Soon after his death his book, *Indian Tales* , written years earlier for his children, was published. These classic and comic tales, which Jaime illustrated, were about Coyote Old Man, the Trickster—who is prominent in Indian folklore of California and Nevada.

In later years, all of Jaime's previously unpublished work, both fiction and non-fiction—save for the mysteriously missing manuscript on the Chinese language—were published by Bob Callahan of the Turtle Island Press in Berkeley, financed largely by Nancy.

Deserted Arborlado Cooper house in Little Sur. It was here that artist Elwood Graham had his easel knocked over again and again. Were ghosts responsible? — Photo by author

XII.

The Second Celtic Twilight

Stories of nature spirits haunting the Coast have gone back as far as anyone can remember. First there were the fog-ghosts, whom the Indians loved and made friends with. These ghosts were lonely and sad. The Indians went out at night from the Mission to meet them in the woods and cheer them up. When the Franciscan fathers learned of this, they followed them out one night and performed an exorcism. The fog-ghosts, howling, departed and the Indians mourned. According to legend, the Father who performed the exorcism went mad, ran over a cliff and was drowned at sea near Point Lobos.

O ne of the strange things about the Sur is the almost total absence of ghost stories. One would think that in a place where so many things had gone on, there would be "ghosts." Perhaps this is due to the fact that the landscape has been, as it were, wiped clean of the past. Almost none of the old buildings and relics remain. After my mother tore down the old Gilkey house in Mill Creek (Bixby Creek), Harry Hunt tore down the Arborlado Cooper House in Little Sur, then the John B.H. Cooper house on Little Sur hill towards Big Sur. These examples were soon followed by almost everyone on the Coast after the highway went through in 1937. New owners, too, had a lot to do with this. The person who bought the beautiful old historic Sousa ranch house at Garapata Creek not only tore it down but replaced it by a huge grey concrete monstrosity. Old shacks and barns fell apart as did the ruined boat landings, and what time and weather did not do, the forest fires did. There were also floods in canyons such as Mill Creek. Little was left behind except for narcissus, calla lillies, and amaryllis growing by no longer existent door steps.

However, as mentioned at the beginning, there is a distinct feeling of the presence of the vanished Indians in the canyons and mountains of the Sur and there are, in fact, one or two actual ghost stories.

One of these was at Point Lobos. My Russian friend Sonia Ransome and her ranger husband, Pinky Ransome, were living in the old whaler's cabin near the cove at Lobos. Sonia was terribly excited and thrilled to actually be living at Lobos and took walks every day on the forest path, through the beautiful rust-covered cypress and to the rocks where one could see the gulls, cormorants and pelicans and hear the sea lions roaring. However, they had been there only a few days when Sonia discovered the cabin was haunted. Every night, exactly at midnight, a ghost appeared. It was in the form of a shapeless mist; it had no features and it seemed to drift through the room with its feet about a foot above the floor. Sonia inquired around and found that in early times a Spaniard had been murdered there, his body buried under the cabin. Sonia and Pinky left Point Lobos on account of the ghost and a little later she went mad and died at Agnews.

The other ghost story—if it is one—has to do with the vanished Arborlado Cooper house in the Little Sur. One day the artist Elwood Graham had a most peculiar and baffling experience. He set up his easel to paint in front of the house which, in its hey-day, had been elegant and boasted a pink marble fireplace; but now the fireplace was cracked and the bright yellow paint which had adorned the walls of the house hung in loops. The windows were broken and ghostly looking and mordant narcissus grew in enormous, fragrant clusters amongst the weeds by the ruined door step. It was an excellent subject for painting, especially as just behind it was an old apple orchard whose gnarled trees gave forth a shrivelled, wizened, but bright red bitter fruit.

But everything went wrong for Graham that day. A wind came up suddenly and knocked his easel over. He picked it up and set out the paints and brushes again. A second wind sprang up and blew it over. This happened again and again but he stubbornly persisted—especially as, in between the gusts of wind, the day was perfectly calm. Finally he gave up. Irritated, in a foul humor, he left, feeling that something had actually been pushing him away from the house. A Monterey photographer named Russ Cummings had gone along and taken a snapshot of the old house. When it was developed he discerned strange, whitish objects in the film. They were behind the broken windows and were not clearly discernible as human forms; they were amorphous bits of mist.

What were they, ghosts?

Many people had died at the Arborlado Cooper house,

including the entire Gschwend family who had perished, one by one, of tuberculosis; and Frank Cooper, Arborlado's brother, died after being fatally injured in a motor accident on Serra Hill. Perpaps that was why the Coopers left it abandoned after that. But on the other hand, their wonderful big house on the hill leading towards Big Sur, which boasted six bathtubs, had also been left to rack and ruin after Martha Cooper Hughes sold it to Harry Hunt, and there was nothing ghostly about that.

Fairies, too, were reported in the Sur.

In 1939, a group of people connected with the left wing Green Street Theatre in San Francisco were spending the weekend at the Tolerton house at Coastlands. Among them were a glass blower, a union organizer, a milkman, a dancer and a playwright named Ettore Rella. It was the dancer who told the tale.

On their way down a trail through a little canyon, they came to a waterfall and in the spray all of them at once saw a tiny fairy with wings, looking exactly like an illustration out of a children's fairy tale book. It couldn't be—but it was.

Shaken, they returned to San Francisco.

On this account, but more especially because of the numerous fantastic tales that grew up around Point Lobos, my ex-husband, Patrick Wall, wittily labelled the Sur Coast "The Second Celtic Twilight."

Stories of nature spirits haunting the Coast have gone back as far as anyone can remember. First there were the fog-ghosts, whom the Indians loved and made friends with. These ghosts were lonely and sad. The Indians went out at night from the Mission to meet them in the woods and cheer them up. When the Franciscan fathers learned of this, they followed them out one night and performed an exorcism. The fog-ghosts, howling, departed and the Indians mourned. According to legend, the Father who performed the exorcism went mad, ran over a cliff and was drowned at sea near Point Lobos.

Point Lobos, the locale of Stevenson's *Treasure Island* has been the focal point of most of the odd tales. People have reported seeing all manner of nature spirits, varying from beautiful devas (angels) with brilliantly flashing wings to evil, fearsome creatures, with bat-like wings and talons. The sea spirits are reputedly the most dangerous to mankind, for they are always dragging people into the sea and drowning them. They do this not malevolently but playfully. It is true that no one who has ever fallen into the sea at Lobos has been known to be rescued.

And there are haunted groves of cypress trees at Lobos—one in particular where psychics say that the priests of ancient Lemuria still dwell in spirit.

Ella Young, the extraordinary Irish woman who held a seat in Celtic lore at the University of California, created for her by Noel Sullivan, told me that Lobos was a sacred place, one of the most powerful in all of America.

This woman, who was active in the Irish movement in Dublin and was closely associated with Lady Gregory, Yeats, George Russell, Synge and Maud Gonne, came to America when she felt that the magic had left Ireland, or rather, as she put it, "When its Guardians changed." She felt that the magic that had left Ireland could now be found in America; that is why she decided to come here. The authorities detained her at Ellis Island when she first arrived because they heard she believed in fairies, elves and pixies and claimed to see them. They did not want this crazy Irish woman to enter the country; but eventually the Irish Society secured her release.

Ella Young, the extraordinary Irish woman who held the seat in Celtic lore at U.C. Berkeley. She declared Point Lobos to be "the center of psychic force for the entire Pacific Coast."
—Courtesy of the Ansel Adams Foundation.

Ella Young was a fantastic being when I first met her at U.C., where she was giving a lecture on the great Irish mythological hero Cuchulain. This was in 1936, so she must have been in her early eighties. Wearing her purple druidic or bardic robes, with her long white hair flowing and her brilliant blue eyes flashing, she seemed not only young but incredibly and super humanly beautiful. She had an indescribable force or magic about her. One did not feel she was human or on our plane. When in her presence, even sitting in a crowded lecture hall, one felt as though encountering a great wind or something equally elemental. Something much bigger or more impersonal than the human.

But Ella Young had her human side, too, as can be seen in her book of memoirs, *Flowering Dusk.* She had a great wit and was very devoted to cats—and her cats were highly unusual, to say the least.

Gavin Arthur, astrologer and grandson of President Arthur, said she had been the chief Druidess in England in a previous lifetime and saved his life when he was a shipwrecked sailor. Ella, herself, believed she had also been an Egyptian, connected with the Bast cult. (The Cat Goddess.)

Years later when I saw her in Carmel at Dr. Levick's house at Carmel Point I was shocked. Ella was in her nineties and she looked very old indeed. She was sitting in a chair by the window, lifeless, shrivelled; she reminded me of a little brown leaf, curled up and faded and about to disintegrate into the forest floor.

Then she looked at me and began talking and the most extraordinary transformation took place. Once again her blue eyes flashed brilliantly; her face became young and beautiful like that of a deva or a member of the elemental kingdom. There was something incredibly radiant and singing about her and I felt as though some great wind from the sea had entered the room.

The lifeless little old lady had disappeared; in her place stood an ageless being shining as the legendary figures in Irish fairy tales or at Tir-nan-Og, the Gaelic paradise.

First she talked about the cypress trees at Point Lobos.

"They are dying," she said. "And they should be saved. The red rust looks beautiful but is killing them. The Park Service is wrong not to get rid of the red rust; and new trees should be planted and the old ones let go."

She paused. "They are sacred trees," she told me.

I asked her then what she thought and felt about Point Lobos as I had heard she believed in sacred mountains and that there was one at Lobos.

"Point Lobos is the center of psychic force for the entire Pacific Coast," she told me. "There are other sacred mountains, other sacred places, but this is the most powerful. But Point Lobos is not ready to make friends with society yet. Mount Shasta is making friends; other great mountains are making friends;

but not Lobos. That is why people should be careful when they go to Lobos."

"How about the Coast to the south?" I asked. "Down towards the Big Sur? People feel much about this Coast..."

"It is the same thing," she interrupted. "It all comes from Lobos. Point Lobos is the center."

"Beware of the sea spirits at Lobos," she added solemnly. "They do not mean to harm anyone. They are like lion cubs. It is dangerous to play with lion cubs."

She also told me there were fairies at Lobos, and a great deva with beautiful wings who guarded the place. One time, she told me, she had been addressing the P.T.A. in Carmel and told them of the fairies at Lobos. To her horror the 150 women in her audience insisted on immediately going to Point Lobos to look for fairies. They didn't find any.

"But after all," she chuckled, "those marching feet... But there aren't as many fairies here as in Ireland," she added. "Mostly here there are the bigger spirits."

Ella Young paused. "The Indians hold the magic of America. When America taps this magic that the Indians had, then we will have great poetry, great music, great singing. This is also true of Lobos. When the force of Lobos is released, a great thing will happen in America—but Lobos is not ready to make friends yet."

Years later, in the early '60s, wearing Ella Young's deep purple amethyst necklace, I went to Lobos with John Cooke and for several months we did daily meditation there, rain or shine. He was in a wheelchair so I had to push it along the edge of cliffs—yet neither of us feared. Towards the end of this period we began hearing heavenly choirs; the last one, strangely, was in Chinese. Finally we invited the entire meditation group which met at the Carmel Highlands to accompany us to the Sacred Grove, not far from the hidden pyramid that was Stevenson's Spyglass Mountain.

There were seven of us that day—and all seven heard the heavenly choir. It was in English this time. We had not told anyone about the choir in advance.

Susan Porter, who lived at Coastlands at Big Sur, got a strange story about Point Lobos through automatic writing. It was part of the lost continent of Gandalon (supposedly the same as Lemuria) and she said that the people worshipped the sun on pyramid-like peaks at certain times of the day; but when the continent and its people grew wicked, as Atlantis did later, the volcanic activity increased and the priests "reversed the vibration" and caused the continent to sink.

Armine von Tempski, red-haired author of *Born in Paradise*, also of the novels, *Hula* and *Fire*, linked it with Lemuria and said she saw little black people there, three feet high, who were exactly like the extinct Menehunes who had once inhabited the island of Kauai in Hawaii. "It's also very close in feeling to the Chinese mountains," said Armine. "The mountains up in the north above Peking."

The most fascinating legend, however, has to do with the cypress trees.

According to a newspaper account, a Tibetan lama attended the San Francisco Exposition in 1915 and insisted on visiting Point Lobos. He told reporters that there were accounts at Llasa of the sacred seeds from the Monastery Garden which had been carried to this spot by Buddhist missionaries about a thousand years ago. These were cypress trees that grew nowhere else in the world except at Lhasa. There were three Buddhist missionaries (this is recorded in Chinese history books of the period) and they had sailed from the land of Fu-Sang (China) eventually reaching California. After planting the sacred seeds at Point Lobos, along with several near the Seventeen Mile Drive at Pebble Beach, they went down to Mexico, where legends of them remain to this day. The Conquistadores heard the story of the enlightenment of the Buddha under the Boddhi tree to their astonishment and disbelief.

The lama visited the groves at Lobos and declared that these were indeed the same trees found in the Monastery Garden at Llasa and nowhere else on earth.

The late Ed Ricketts, marine biologist and the "Doc" of John Steinbeck's *Cannery Row* felt there was something strange and very sinister about the Coast and Lobos, in which he was not alone, as I heard the same tale from many other sources in one form or another. The essence of it was that people would suddenly feel overshadowed and be seized by a feeling of terror. Once when Ed Ricketts was climbing the mountains above Lobos in the Carmel Highlands with Rich and Tal Lovejoy (Rich was a reporter on the *Monterey Herald*), all three of them were suddenly overcome with terror. A nameless invisible menace seemed about to attack them. They ran all the way down the mountain to the highway where their car was parked, exchanging not a single word, and sped to town.

Ed gave this phenomenon a name. He called it The Terror.

I might not have quite believed Ed if I had not had an identical experience in the company of Frank and Marjory Lloyd of Carmel. (Both were editors of the *Carmel Pine Cone*.) They came down to Mill Creek to visit the old deserted limekiln, three miles up the canyon, and we got there about noon. It was a hot day. We sat in the blazing sun, feeling relaxed and happy, looking at the old deserted houses with their broken-down stair cases and cracked windows gaping blank as broken teeth. (The Italian limekiln workers had once lived here, several hundred of them. The Japanese, however, had a village of their own on the opposite side of the creek, the walls of their cabins papered with yellowed Japanese newspapers.) Above us was the huge cracked limekiln oven. Bees were buzzing. The atmosphere seemed peaceful. We were hungry and about to open our paper bags to eat our picnic lunch when suddenly, all three of us, without saying a word to each other, rose and started back down the trail. We walked fast; we didn't run, but we felt like running. I, for one, was terrified. We did not speak until we had safely reached the road near the

Cypress trees at Lobos. Originally from the Monastery garden at Llasa. According to a Tibetan lama, the sacred seeds were carried here by three Buddhist missionaries from Fu-Sang (China) in 1000 A.D.
—Ink drawing by author

wooden county bridge where our car was parked three miles down canyon. We killed a rattlesnake on the way, because it was on the path (in the shade!) and about to strike. We did not know what had frightened us, only that we had been terrified. Something nameless had threatened us and we had fled.

That is why I believed Ed Ricketts.

On the whole, however, I found the Coast benign. I think that was because I lived there and was close to its spirit. As I said earlier, one had to get to know it, to make friends with it. And, also, even if one lived there, one had to approach it cautiously. One never entered a wood without first asking permission and waiting until one felt one had received it. This was especially true at Point Lobos.

Charlie and Alta Bixby Gregg on horseback on part of the old Bixby ranch on Bixby Mountain. They left the Coast soon after the war started, never to return.
—Collection of Elizabeth Hogue Van Der Pleough

XIII.

Stalked by a Lynx

Ronald Colman, the movie actor, arrived in the late 1920s and bought a ranch below Anderson Creek. Then came Lathrop Brown, a close friend of Franklin D. Roosevelt, his roommate at Harvard, best man at his wedding, and assistant secretary of the Interior during World War I. Other comers included avant garde writer Henry Miller, a refugee from occupied France, Jock and Isadora Stevens, Emil White, Hugh O'Neill, Gilbert Niemann and Nicholas Roosevelt of the Teddy Roosevelt branch.

I n the summer of 1938 when I came home from Reed College, I found the family living in one of our cabins—the only one that had modern plumbing, a bathtub, and running hot water. In the days when my father was away, my 14-year-old brother, Willy, (usually called "Beans") took to shooting the numerous black widow spiders with his 22 rifle. Daddy may have wondered but never asked about the bullet holes in the cabin walls.

Rainbow Lodge was no more. It had ceased to exist on July 3, 1937, when the old glorified wagon road was abandoned after the ceremony at Bixby Creek Bridge when old Doc Roberts cut the ribbon officially opening the new highway to tourist traffic. A portion of the old road still exists (and does to this day) from Bixby Creek (formerly Mill Creek) to the mouth of Big Sur River, now the Andrew Molera State Park, but the tourists never noticed it. Rainbow Lodge, like Camp Idlewild in the Little Sur, had gone out of existence. Everyone kept their eyes glued to the new spectacular highway.

Life had changed entirely since I had left a year earlier.

My parents had discovered the supposedly extinct southern sea-otter in March of 1938 and thousands of tourists had come flocking to our place, at that time called the Stone House, at the northern end of Rainbow Bridge (Bixby Bridge), to view the otters through the telescope on our big observation porch.

I was not interested in dealing with the tourists and had been looking forward to a quiet summer of writing and painting.

The canyon seemed eerie and silent without a single car coming down the road and I had the terrifying experience, when there alone one day, of being stalked by a big Canadian tufted lynx. People laugh at me when I say I was in danger from a lynx, but I well remember the time a man riding horseback up Serra Hill was killed by a bobcat who dropped down on his shoulders from a tree above him.

The family was up at the Stone House, including my brother who was on vacation from high school for the summer, where my mother was serving sandwiches, salad and chili beans to tourists. This was a restaurant and stone building my father had built of native granite lined with redwood from Big Creek Mill in 1932 when the highway (and bridge) were still under construction.

The author on Bixby Landing in 1944.
—Photo by Brett Weston

I got bored in the cabin so I decided to go for a walk and, just as I was entering a thicket of alders and cottonwood near the old abandoned fish hatchery, I suddenly had the feeling that there was something overhead. I stopped in my tracks and looked up. There was a huge lynx, flexing his muscles to pounce. My last experience with a lynx had been at age 11 when I looked out my window to see one consuming a big wild rabbit. "Crunch, crunch, crunch," it went.

I turned in a flash and started walking slowly, slowly, slowly—as slowly as possible—back to the cabin. I knew better than to run as the lynx would have attacked me at once. The trick was to deceive him into thinking I did not notice his existence. But above all, I had to school myself to feel no fear, for he would have smelled the odor of fear. (This is, by the way, not an easy thing to do.) It was a long way back to the cabin, or so it seemed under the circumstances. I had to cross a five acre vacant field after leaving the thicket. Finally I was close enough to the front door of the cabin that I dared to make a run for it. I made it just in time with the lynx behind

me. I banged the door shut in his face. He was not about to give up, and for the next hour circled the cabin, around and around, trying to find a way in. Fearing he might be able to get down the chimney somehow or pry open one of the back windows (they were not securely nailed) I built a fire in the woodstove and set a big pan of water boiling on it. I had no gun, but I could throw scalding water on him if he succeeded in getting in. Then suddenly, a car came down the hill. I could not believe it, as cars no longer travelled

William "Beans" Sharpe, age 17, at the Stone House. A gifted artist, sculptor and cartoonist who was killed in the 8th Air Force as first pilot of a bomber in 1944. I called him Willy.
— Photo by author

this road. A red-haired young man was getting out of his truck. He took his rifle and shot the lynx—an incredible happening, since this was the only vehicle that had come down the hill in several days. It seemed a miracle. When he saw the lynx circling the cabin and smoke coming from the chimney he knew that the occupant was in trouble and therefore took action.

It was on account of this quite bizzare episode that my mother decided we should leave the canyon and move up to the Stone House. We were never to return to the canyon again.

Bixby Inn, showing the unconsonant addition (office and kitchen) where we all lived after I was stalked by a lynx in the lonely deserted canyon. Bixby Inn, too, closed when war
came in 1941.   —Postcard, collection of Pat Hathaway

There were no real sleeping accommodations at the Stone
House (later called Bixby Inn, and after the war Gallatin's, and
finally The Crocodile's Tail) but my father and brother slept in
the earthen-floored basement, and my mother and I shared
the office which we turned into a bedroom, removing the
office furniture and files. Later, because I had undulant fever,
my mother moved out to sleep on a glassed in portion of the
observation porch. This took a great deal of valiance during
the winter storm season.

Here in the daytime, hundreds of tourists poured in to view
the sea otters through my father's telescope at 10 cents apiece.
My father had re-discovered the supposedly extinct southern
sea otter in March of 1938. In 1841, Captain John B.R. Cooper
had reported that there was not a single otter to be found on
the entire Coast between Fort Ross and below Big Sur. (The
Mexican province and the Russians were defending
themselves against hundreds of foreign poachers.) One day
my father saw some peculiar looking sea animals offshore,
playing and floating in the kelp beds as he was gazing through
his telescope. He called my mother who got out his

Rainbow Bridge, opened to tourist traffic in 1937, brought an end to an entire way of life. Rainbow Lodge was no more. The real changes were not distinctly felt, however, until after World War II.   —Postcard, collection of Pat Hathaway

binoculars. It occurred to him that they might be sea-otters, but how could they be? The southern sea-otter had supposedly been extinct for 107 years. In great excitement, he phoned Hopkins Marine Station but was met with disbelief. It took three phone calls before he could persuade them to come down to investigate. Then there was great excitement in all the newspapers, including headlines on the front page of the *San Francisco Call Bulletin*. In reality, it was claimed, the scientists at Hopkins Marine Station had known of the existence of the southern sea otter all along but did not want to let it out to the public for fear of poachers. Stiff laws, however, were immediately passed to protect the sea otters.

That summer, once we had moved to the Stone House, I was astonished one day to look out the window and see a boat with men in it riding close to the sea otters and taking pictures of them. This was the famous John Hancock expedition.

I still missed the canyon, but I never went down there alone, not after my brush with the lynx. The house had ceased to exist in 1934, just four years earlier. My father had gone off on a trip (he was crazy about trips) and we were living in one of the cabins, as we had been away from Rainbow Lodge for an entire year while Mother was in the hospital and the house had fallen into disrepair. My mother didn't want to fix it up again. It was huge, a woman-killer and she nad never wanted to live in it in the first place. It had seven bedrooms, a huge living room, a huge dining room, a second living room, a cavernous kitchen, a nursery and a sleeping porch.

Howard G. Sharpe looking through his telescope at the sea otters he rediscovered off Bixby Landing. Photo excerpted from the May 14, 1938, pictorial spread on the otter find in *The San Francisco Call Bulletin.*
— Courtesy Friends of the Sea Otter

One morning Frida ordered Bosco Bryan, the hired man, and my 11-year-old brother, Willy, to go to work with wrecking bars and tear it down. They did so. Although the house was enormous, they got it down in a couple of days. Cleverly they left the front of the house standing, like a Hollywood facade. People coming down the road thought the house was still there. It was months before my father discovered it was gone, as we had rented a house in Carmel by the time he returned from his trip. One day he drove down to the canyon to have a look at the water system. The restaurant was supplied with water by a hydraulic dam down in the creek and our electricity was from a kohler plant, like those used by the local purse seiners.

Daddy came back to town to say, "Why, Frida, the house is gone!"

Frida G. Sharpe returning to Bixby Inn from a trek into the wilderness to gather her favorite flower, the fragant wild spikenard also known as false Solomon's seal. They bloom only in the spring when the wild lilac, trilium, and the pink blossoming wild currant too are out. The time was April, 1941.
(Note: Photo was badly damaged by a flood in 1983.)
—Photo by Flavia Flavin Edgren

Mother lighted a cigarette —slowly. "Well, what do you know," she dryly remarked.

The subject was dropped and never brought up again.

For months the house had been a bone of contention. Now the argument was ended. As Frida was to say years later, "Act—don't talk."

Ranch life did not change overnight in the Sur but the changes that happened at the Sharpe ranch were reflected, in one way or another, all up and down the Coast. And naturally we got closer to our neighbors down in the Big Sur and even at Lucia than we had before the highway was built. Now it took us little time to get there. Several of the old-timers opened restaurants and motels along the highway, including our neighbor, West Smith, who had a bar at Westmere. During limekiln days he had had a bar in Mill Creek Canyon, catering to the limekiln workers. But most of the newer businesses were down in the Big Sur, including the Post's who opened a restaurant (and dude ranch) at Rancho Sierra Mar. Then, too, there were two state parks, which brought many visitors to the area: Point Lobos Reserve and Pfeiffer Big Sur State Park. Johnny Pfeiffer sold most of his land to the State of California in 1934 for $750,000 and Alexander M. Allen sold Point Lobos for $600,000. Pfeiffer's Resort — which had started up quite accidentally in 1910 when Mrs. Pfeiffer found a man beating a mule with a picket and ordered him to stop, and said that from now on she would charge him and his men for food and lodging as well as for feeding the mules. (This greatly upset John Pfeiffer who had grown up in the pattern of Spanish hospitality. "Whoever comes is welcome.") "We nearly split the blankets over that," Florence Pfeiffer remarked in her journal.

Pfeiffer's Resort had closed down, replaced by the slick and modern Big Sur Lodge. People could camp at Big Sur but not at Point Lobos.

Frida Sharpe.   —Collection of author

Back in the hills, however, there were a few people living as they had for decades, raising cattle and riding horseback, cooking on woodstoves and lighting their houses with kerosene lamps, and when they were out of kerosene, tallow candles. The pancake batter went on from year to year, tasting better and better as time went on. Among these old timers were Charlie and Alta Bixby Gregg who lived up near the top of Bixby mountain on part of the old Bixby ranch. The old house had been bought by the Horace Hogues who later left it abandoned. Alta was the daughter of Charlie Bixby for whom the mountain and boat landing and eventually the canyon and bridge were named. The Greggs had never in their entire lives owned a spring wagon as their ranch was accessible only by trail. Once a week they rode down from Bixby Mountain on horseback to get the mail and a few scant supplies — bacon, coffee, sugar, maybe some flour or beans — from the mail stage when it stopped at Bixby Creek Bridge. In pre-highway days, the ride to get the mail had not been a very long one;

West Smith who had a bar at Mill Creek during the raucous limekiln days. Later he had a bar at Westmere, the Smith family ranch house at Rocky Creek. The old house burned down; nothing is left but cypress trees.   —Photo by author

they had only to get down to the wagon road at the top of Serra Hill to pick it up. But now it took several hours. The Greggs had seen so little of people up there on the mountain that they were shy of the outside world and it was with considerable effort that my mother succeeded in enticing them into the restaurant for free coffee and conversation while waiting for the mail stage. They were like wild deer. Gradually they loosened up and began to enjoy these expeditions which gave them something to look forward to — some human contact. We became great friends.

The Greggs were the only people living on the Coast who used the horse as their only means of transportation after the highway went through. Gradually everyone purchased motor cars. But the Greggs had no road to their ranch and besides, as Charlie said, "I wouldn't take one of those new-fangled contraptions as a free gift."

Horses were more human and companionable. One could communicate with a horse, Charlie felt.

To everyone's surprise, Johnny Pfeiffer was the very first to buy a motor car. (My father and the J.B.R. Coopers had always had them, but Pfeiffer was the first of the pioneer families to buy one.) In wagon road days, everyone had been warned in advance when Johnny Pfeiffer made the trip to town in his spring wagon. He travelled straight down the road and would give way to no one. He refused to get close to the precipitous canyon edge. Neither would he back up a hill nor wait even if a whole line of vehicles was coming along behind him. No, Johnny Pfeiffer was a character all right, and people simply stayed home when they heard he was coming up the road from Big Sur. If he had been such a demon with the spring wagon, what would he be with an automobile? It did not bear thinking of. To everyone's amazement, Johnny Pfeiffer proved to be a good and entirely safe driver, keeping to his own lane of the road and adhering strictly to the traffic rules. He never once tried to hog the road or had an accident.

The highway also inevitably brought newcomers to the Coast—not prioneer cattle ranchers or woodsmen but "city folk." (In the beginning, the Sharpe family was also referred to as "city folk"; but one day Corbett Grimes came by and found my mother hoeing her own vegetable garden. From then on we were accepted.) The first of the newcomers was the colony at Coastlands established in 1926. They had a meeting house or club house called the Trails Club built by the indispensible Sam Trotter. Later this place was bought as a gift for Rita Hayworth by Orson Welles's business manager, but she never saw it and later it was bought by the Bill Fassetts who made it their home while they established Nepenthe, the famous restaurant below.

Ronald Colman, the movie actor, arrived in the late 1920s and bought a ranch below Anderson Creek. Then came Lathrop Brown, a close friend of Franklin D. Roosevelt, his roommate at Harvard, best man at his wedding, and assistant secretary of the Interior during World War I. (At this time my father's first cousin, William G. Sharpe, was Ambassador to France.) Other comers included *avant garde* writer Henry Miller, a refugee from occupied France, Jock and Isadora Stevens (she was a pianist and he did ceramics), Emil White, Hugh O'Neill, and Gilbert Niemann. Another arrival was Nicholas Roosevelt of the Teddy Roosevelt branch. He raised roses on Partington Ridge. After Pearl Harbor, most of the artists including Jean "Yanko" Varda moved away, but Henry Miller stayed on and it was while on Partington that he wrote his fantastically humorous *A Devil in Paradise* as well as *The Big Sur and the Oranges of Heironymous Bosch.*

Charlie Gregg's outhouse blew down during a storm in 1942 with him in it, and although he was uninjured the experience shook him up. The outhouse, on a trail several hundred feet from the house, commanded a fine view of the Coast thousands of feet below. It had rested upon an oak tree and since the oak tree had been blown down during the storm it could not be rebuilt—not in the same spot.

Charlie was too old to change. He left the Coast shortly after this. Charlie was unhappy without his old outhouse and, in addition, he and Alta were getting old; they had arthritis and most of the neighbors had moved away. It was lonely and even dangerous there on the mountain. There was no one to come to their rescue, as my brother "Beans" used to do, during winter storms.

Frank Post began keeping a diary after the war started. His son-in-law, Steve Yaeger, was away in the Army; his little grandson, Peter, had died at the age of four; and very few cars came down the highway now that the war had closed the road to tourist traffic. The few resorts had been forced to shut down—including Bixby Inn.

Hardly anyone every stopped at Loma Vista Inn where Frank Post, his wife Annie and his daughter Alice held down the fort. Annie, née Annie Pate of Little Sur, had been one of the revelers at dances at *El Sur* half a century earlier where she had met Frank Post. Post's thoughts turned more and more to the old days, to the time when his father was alive and young pioneers, now in their graves, were first coming down the Coast trail. In his diary he wrote strict instructions for his funeral; he wanted to be cremated; he wanted no preacher, no sermon; he was to be buried at the ranch. "I don't want to be buried in the city of the dead. Let no one gaze on my cold features."

He was a natural poet. Examples of his style may be found in the following entries from his diary which he commenced in 1943, after Steve, his son-in-law, went into the Army.

April 4. Rake up, cut grass, dumped it over the slope. The sunset shone on the mountains until it dropped out of sight beyond the horizon. Heavy wind all day from the north. Alice got a letter from Steve today. Stated in letter that it's the first time in his life that he ever knew what it was to be homesick. Dear Steve, I feel for you. As I never was away from home, I am a stranger to that malady, home sickness. But I've worked in places, one place in particular, where I thought of my home in the mountains and longed to be there than working in a place that I had such a dislike.

Another entry was made April 9.

Hoed the strawberry patch and grass along the back road and the onion bed. Quite a wind from the north but not cold this morning. I could see from the kitchen window the sun's ray as it touched the mountain's rugged crest Mount Manuel. At this writing, the mountain above is shrouded in darkness and the mountain lion is on the hunt for the helpless deer.

But Uncle Frank's most moving entry was his last one, in which he referred to his Great Keeper who kept watch over him and had saved him from death so many times in the wild Coast hills. The entry was made on June 22, 1945, the summer solstice.

June 22. Today is the longest day of the year so they tell me. Am now coming to the end of my writing in this diary. What I've been writing in this from day to day it don't amount to much, mostly every day events. But thanks to the Good Lord that has taken care of us, and to me in the long years that I have been in His care, no doubt in my day; more so in hiking through the mountains along the craggy rough sea shore in all probability death hovered so near and ready to grab me but I was not aware of its presence, but thanks to my Caretaker that has always been by my side night and day... Will now close. Thanks again to the Good Lord for health, lots to eat, a good bed and a nice home. How thankful I should be.

As I read Uncle Frank Post's diary, in his clear, beautiful, impeccable handwriting, I remembered the strange escape from death my mother, brother and I had had years back when we were walking down the old landing trail (originally a wagon road) to our cabin in the canyon from the Stone House one night. Father was in town with the car, and our flashlight had gone out. There was no moon. The dog was with us, but he could see no more clearly than we. We could not see a step in front of us. It was black as pitch. The trail was rough, over-hung a precipice, and there was stubble and clumps of grass underfoot. But there was no trouble after all. A light appeared behind us and guided us all the way home. It was like a huge flashlight. When we got safely to the door of our cabin, it went out. We opened the door and lighted the kerosene lamp.

That is why I feel to this day that those of us who were close to the spirit of this wild and beautiful land found it benign and ever protective—not the opposite.

After all, old Frank Post, the first old timer to be born in the Sur, did not die as soon as he had anticipated, and so he quit writing in his diary when he son-in-law, Steven Yaeger, came home from the war. He lingered on until he was 92 years of age, getting up every morning to watch the dawn coming up over Mount Manuel (named for the Indian Manuel Innocenti) as he sat in the kitchen drinking coffee; he went on chopping wood and doing small chores about the ranch and even went out hunting for cougars when they preyed on the horses and cattle. Mingled with his sadness, his nostaglia for the past, his love for his parents whom he missed, was his deep love for the beauty of the land he lived in and which seemed alive to him — even as it did to me. The end came in 1951. His wife, Annie, had preceded him.

One by one the old timers were going; Johnny Pfeiffer, Florence Pfeiffer, Sam Trotter, Joe Post, Frank Post, Alvin

Dani, Corbett Grimes, Frida Sharpe, West Smith.   And Robinson Jeffers, too, died in 1962.   Una had pre-deceased him. They seemed to be falling like old trees in the forest.   They were being culled out.

***

Evil spirits, shadows, the darkness of tragedy, these things existed mainly for Outsiders and were but shadows, not really real—certainly not for the Indians nor for the early pioneers nor for old Frank Post.   To him the spirit of the Sur Coast was ever shining, ever splendid and beneficient—as it was to his handsome brother Joe.

The landscape itself will always remain stronger than the people who came and went on it and cannot be touched.   The last time I went down to the site of Rainbow Lodge I found no evidence of our existence, not even a rose bush or a clump of amaryllis.   And the field, the clearing, had grown over with willows.   The willows had crept in from the creek and obliterated all traces of human invasion.

Like my mother, I felt glad of it—not sad.

Yet one has one's memories.   And so will the voices sound forever—John Gilkey riding up the old Coast road, his auburn hair rippling behind him in the wind, saying, "This is a free life, not crowded..."

RAINBOW LODGE PROPERTIES - SHOWING RAINBOW BRIDGE, 15 M. SOUTH OF CARMEL, AND MONTEREY, CALIF.

The stone house was built by H. G. Sharpe in 1932 But no one drove across the bridge until the highway was opened in 1937. —Courtesy of Pat Hathaway

XIV.

Postscript

All the Ghosts Have Vanished

Appreciation of Bridge's Beauty

"A Wild Coast and Lonely"

---

*Somehow it had never appeared so
lovely before, as though a special patina
of beauty lay on the land because this
was the best — and the last.*

Postscript

I shall never forget that last fall on the Big Sur Coast before Pearl Harbor. Somehow it had never appeared so lovely before, as though a special patina of beauty lay on the land because this was the best — and the last. Never had the sunsets been more crimson, the sea so shining like glass, the hawks

and the cormorants and seagulls flying and even an eagle or two. The old stag sneered down at the tourists from the hill above our stone house on the cliff until hunting season began — of which he seemed always to have foreknowledge.

My mother and brother were as aware as I of the prescient splendor upon the shining land and we all sensed its meaning.

Willy (Beans) had grown so lean and lithe and manly in his 18th year. He had been managing the ranch and driving the truck since age 14 — and he went out on solitary 100 mile hikes in the Ventana wilderness (they took him only 3 days) with his sleeping bag, his canteen, his backpack, his gun and his dog.

We had fought as children, but once in our teens we discovered a world in common: literature, music, art, philosophy and even architecture. Willy was an artist and a sculptor, but he wanted to become an architect and build houses with curves — instead of straight cubicles in rectangles and squares.

On that last afternoon before it all ended we stood on the observation porch overlooking the sea, our beach and the mountains to the south. Our shining, massive hills were all cougar-colored, the way they get in the fall.

And Willy said, "Rosy — we can't go beyond this, you know. There is nothing to strive for — nothing to attain. This beauty is perfect and whole."

I had to agree.

World War II was upon us and we felt its breath.

All the Ghosts Have Vanished

(Originally appeared in **The Herald Weekend Magazine,** September 21, 1986.)

I was not at all prepared for it. I had expected to feel the usual pangs of sadness at encountering the empty field where our ranch house once stood — a field which we had once planted in potatoes and the gophers ate them. I expected to find the rose bush still blooming on the vanished doorstep of what had once been our back porch, and the evocative pink amaryllis and flaming red canna lilies down by the creek, below the ancient redwood with its old frayed rope still hanging. I had expected to be not only nostalgic but somewhat resentful that I no longer owned the place and was but a visitor there, an intruder in what to me (inwardly) was still my own land.

I had grown up here in Mill Creek (Bixby Creek) and to me it was my Home Place — as old-timers down the Sur Coast always referred to it.

It had been over 15 years since I had been to Bixby Canyon. Although in my 20 years of exile from the Monterey Peninsula I made a trip home at least once a year, I avoided the old stamping grounds like the plague. I was afraid of memories.

But somehow this feeling had passed and so I went down there to visit friends who lived in the canyon.

To my astonishment the empty field no longer existed nor did the rose bush. There were no amaryllis or canna lilies, either near the creek or at the site of our many cabins that had burned down in the forest fire of 1941. The frayed rope no longer hung from the redwood tree — but the ancient tree was still growing and growing, getting taller, verdant, although obviously graying with the years. It was a solitary tree. It had always been solitary.

Aside from the tree, and another younger one I had planted across the road from the house when I was a small child, there was nothing, absolutely nothing to remind me of the past — and, most striking of all, there was absolutely nothing to give evidence of our existence there or, in fact, of any prior human existence whatever.

The willows had taken over!

They had crept onto the field (all five acres of it) from the creek and simply overwhelmed it. Man and his puny efforts had been vanquished by the wilderness. One part of me rejoiced; another part of me found this sinister and reminded me of the feelings I used to have as a child being surrounded by a vast inimical wilderness from which we were hardly protected by the frail wooden walls of our isolated ranch house.

On moonlight nights, the coyotes dared to come down into the clearing from the mesa above and even howl there, sometimes circling our house expectantly — and tufted lynxes and mountain lions, too, came close to the house, not frightened of us or our domestic animals.

Our two big dogs, Roddy and Carlo, one a big collie, the other a shepherd, came off the worse for an encounter with a lion under the bridge. My father went down with a gun to aid them, but was forced to retreat.

All of this was gone.

The willows had taken over.

I was reminded of the strange tales of Algernon Blackwood, especially one called "The Willows," in which the willows, like those here, had vanquished — nay, eradicated — man.

We proceeded down the canyon on the little dirt automobile road my father had built in the mid '20s to visit John and Claudia Ruster, old friends from Carmel, who had bought a piece of the ranch from my father in 1952. They had a lovely house of native creek rock and adobe halfway between what used to be the clearing (and before that the site of our ranch house) and the beach. The beach, to my disappointment, was no longer accessible. A giant winter storm had created a huge lagoon that stemmed the canyon from side to side. One could only get down to the ocean by climbing along a trail on the high cliff.

But I came away feeling happy and at peace — as though the ghosts, our ghosts, that is to say, had been driven away. And I remembered my mother saying in the fall of 1941 after the forest fire had destroyed everything we had ever built there, "Isn't it beautiful, wiped all clean again? Now the Earth is free." And in the spring the golden poppies came out profusely, as they always do after a big forest fire, and the burnt redwood grove up on the hill was turning reddish brown with touches of green leafing through and somehow looked quite Chinese. I could now see what mother meant. And this, too, was a feeling often expressed by Robinson Jeffers.

***

I went down again after Christmas with my children and grandchildren and there were nine of us in the party descending on the helpless Rusters, who most graciously gave us coffee, tea, lemonade and cookies. The four elves (the grandchildren) were marvelously good and 2-year-old Jennifer was not at all afraid of the Rusters' two big dogs, who are very spoiled because they had rescued John and Claudia from the flood that raged through the canyon in the early spring of 1983. The two dogs woke them by jumping on their bed at 4 a.m. and would not desist until they had aroused the two deeply sleeping people; and then John discovered, by flashlight since the power had failed, that water was already coming into their room. They had to escape through the top of a dutch door. The dogs, who were only puppies then, joined them in making their way through the torrent to a neighbor's house on a hill slightly above the canyon floor — high enough to be above flood water. When the waters did not subside, they moved into town for a few days. On their return, they found that 16 inches of water had been in their house and much was ruined, the most important of which were irreplaceable family photos that they kept in a box on the floor.

I sympathized, for that very same year — in January, 1983 — I had gone through exactly the same thing on the Russian River and lost most of my family photos, including old pictures of the ranch at Bixby. (Two feet of water were in my home and I lost about $5,000 worth of household goods; but this part didn't seem to matter.)

In my day, when my father had a tourist resort called Rainbow Lodge there, the place was called Mill Creek and so it appears in the Jeffers poems. (It had once been the location of a lumber mill that shipped out tanbark, shakes and pickets.)

I left the canyon that day after tea with the Rusters on December 28, the day after my 66th birthday, feeling joyful at last. One does not need to own the land to love it, know it and be a part of it. In reality, as the Indians believe, the land belongs to no one but we to it.

It is our Mother Earth.

And how truly marvelous it seemed that the ghosts of past and of all human pasts had vanished from the land, leaving it free and untrammelled and essentially untouched. It is filled now only with its present loveliness, the eternal beauty of things and that of the life to come which will be, essentially, ever the same for as long as the stars remain in their places.

Appreciation of Bridge's Beauty

(Originally appeared in **The Herald Weekend Magazine,** October 18, 1987.)

The celebration of the 50th anniversary of the Coast Highway brought back to me how sad, angry and upset I was when I first heard about the bridge which was to span our canyon and end forever our glorious freedom and solitude. People would be peering down at us from the bridge above our beach, where we were accustomed to bathing in the surf and running up and down the strand in the nude. Now we would have to don bathing suits.

My father, although he was the principle nudist of the family, was exultant. The State of California had offered him more than $4,000 for an easement across our property at Bixby Creek, and he visualized making millions of dollars from the tourist trade.

Rainbow Lodge, our resort down in the canyon, was a strictly seasonal business. Everything shut up tight as a drum after Labor Day. But a highway connecting the Monterey Peninsula with San Luis Obispo Country beaches and Los Angeles to the south — that was something else. The hitherto isolated and lonely coast would now be a part of the world.

He happily used the state money to build a place called the Stone House at the northern end of what was to be Bixby Creek Bridge but was called Rainbow Bridge at first, after our resort. Stone House was made of granite hauled up from the beach below and lined with redwood from the Big Creek mill near Lucia.

By 1932 my father had opened it to the public, as the highway had already been cut that far, leaving the winding old wagon road forever a thing of the past. Now tourists came down to the Stone House and looked at the view from my father's big observation porch. He had a gas pump at the site, and a country-store showcase in which he displayed fishing tackle, bait, candy bars, soft drinks, cigarettes, canned food and such. As he didn't know how to cook, he offered no other refreshments.

I hated tourists and loathed all this. I was 10 years old in 1929 when work on the highway started (with convict labor), and even though it was fun when all the engineers made their headquarters at our ranch house I was unhappy to see the changes. I liked things the way they were. When Labor Day came and the tourists departed, I was relieved and joyous. We would go around and pick up the beer cans, soda bottles, candy papers and other litter that the traveling public left behind and once again things would return to normal. The singing birds — wild canaries, beautiful orange-winged orioles, purple finches — the barking of foxes, the howling of coyotes, even the scream of a bobcat. The people were gone and nature triumphed again.

And when spring came, the canyon turned pink with blossoming wild currant and the mountains blue-violet with wild lilac. I sensed that the world I knew and loved would vanish with the coming of the highway. Clearly I belonged to an earlier century.

I didn't want to go down to the beach once the concrete pilings began going up. It was dangerous, too, as chunks of concrete often fell, or were hurled down into the canyon; once my brother and I were almost hit. Because of the presence of the convicts, I was no longer free to walk unchaperoned up the trail to the Brazil ranch on the mesa above us, nor to gather loganberries and wild huckleberries from our own part of the mesa.

One day my father took my brother, William, and me for a walk up the steep trail from the canyon to inspect the bridge under construction. We stopped en route to pick loganberries.

Then, on Brazil property where Tony did his ploughing with horses before the spring planting, we came upon a crew of convicts working with pick and shovel — preparing the ground, I suppose, for the bulldozers. My father, gun at his hip in his usual military way, led his little company of two young privates through the mass of sullen-faced men and I was feeling rather sorry for them until I suddenly became aware of something quite terrible. A pre-adolescent girl, I was beginning to develop breasts and the convicts, to a man, were staring at them.

From the south piling of the bridge a cable and narrow catwalk led to the other side of the canyon. When my father said we had to cross it, despite my terror of heights I had to agree. It seemed the lesser of two evils to walk across the catwalk than to go back through the sea of staring convicts. To this day I can't remember doing it. I only know that somehow I did get to the other side and there was a steel cable to hang onto.

This expedition made me hate the bridge more than ever.

Then came the highway cuts north of the bridge — the beautiful copper-colored earth sliced by huge bulldozers. To me it seemed like cutting into human flesh. Robinson Jeffers expressed the same feeling in his poem, "Thurso's Landing," which was published about this time. The poet was even then my mentor and great hero, perhaps because his feelings about the land seemed so akin to mine.

It would be another five years before the highway was completed between Carmel and San Luis Obispo, some 135 miles to the south. In the meantime, my father at once catered to and glared at the tourists, whom he resented as much as I did.

***

The presence of the engineers at our ranch house was, to me, the one redeeming feature of this major construction project. Life became, instead of solitary, a continuous party. These were rum-running days, and we soon became accustomed to the habits of the rum-runners and the revenue boats that pursued them. The rum-runners would dump the cargo in various coves and caves along the Big Sur coast and weights would keep it underwater for three days; then it would bob to the surface.

One of the favorite dumping places was the cave at Bixby Creek, where

Woodcut etching of Bixby Creek done by the author.

we went for abalones. My father and the state engineers, including chief engineer W. B. Albertson, kept a close watch. Whenever a cargo was dumped offshore they would wait three days and then go down to retrieve it. Our house was filled with cases of bootleg whiskey, gin, rum, brandy, vodka, etc.

My father had been a teetotaler prior to Prohibition. Now, like so many others, he took to drink — largely perhaps because it was forbidden. He also made home brew in huge vats in the kitchen, and I shall never forget the night there was a tremendous explosion in a bedroom upstairs. Three hundred bottles of beer had blown up all at once!

As I look back on it now, I suppose I should have been

shocked, but I was having too good a time. It was fun when all the adults were so enjoying themselves with poker and booze. The fact that my maternal grandmother was head of the Women's Christian Temperance Union in Santa Clara County never crossed my mind, nor that my other grandmother was a personal friend of the prohibitionist leader Carrie Nation.

When the highway was completed I refused to attend the ceremony on July 3, 1937, when Dr. John L. D. Roberts — whose dream the new scenic highway had been — cut the ribbon in front of our Stone House to allow the tourists to use the bridge for the first time. I didn't even want to read newspaper accounts of the ceremony. I loved old Doc Roberts, who had been the Coast's only doctor (he started his practice there in 1887) and I knew him quite well, due to my friendship with his grandson whom I had met at Monterey High School, but even so...

No, I would have nothing to do with the highway or the bridge that everyone was praising so highly. They said it was a miracle in concrete and steel and the most beautiful and largest reinforced concrete steel suspension bridge in the world (also the highest) except for one in the south of France. I was blind to its beauty.

I sat and sulked in a little studio in Carmel during the opening ceremony for the highway, then called the Carmel-San Simeon Highway, later the Roosevelt Highway and now State Highway 1.

Although I lived in the Stone House (after we had changed its name to Bixby Inn) for three years prior to World War II, I still failed to see the beauty of the bridge; I was totally hung up on the past. However, I did notice one thing: The highway had saved the beauty of the coast from intrusion, rather than the opposite.

Where in the past the old wagon road had wandered in and out of every redwood canyon, the tourists who sped along the new highway never entered them. So the foxes and bobcats increased, as did the wild birds, the wild flowers, the trees and the bushes. The canyons were far more protected now than they had been in pre-highway days — far more private, far more silent. One could hear the wind, the beating surf and the occasional bark of a sea otter or a seal. The tourists kept to the highway.

And the highway itself had points which I was forced to observe. The ugly gorge cuts began to subdue and soften, looking less like raw-cut bleeding flesh, and succulents were planted. Then, too — to a great extent due to my mother's efforts with the board of supervisors and the County Planning Commission — there were no billboards, no hot dog stands, no flashy buildings along this undeniably spectacular highway. I well remember the day my family went to a meeting of the planning commission in two separate cars. My father in his gray Oldsmobile, was accompanied by a lawyer; my mother, brother and I drove in the Ford pickup. And my mother's eloquent speeches on behalf of preserving the natural beauty of the highway won the day.

Doc Roberts, who founded the city of Seaside and had been a member of the supervisors for 20 years, also was in favor of keeping out big, ugly signs and undue commercialism.

This was my mother's signal accomplishment: cooperating with the Monterey County Board of Supervisors in maintaining the beauty of what is generally acknowledged today to be the most beautiful scenic coastal highway in the world. Sometimes it is compared to the Amalfi Drive in Italy, but it is more dramatic, the huge hills more massive and sculptured.

In 1985 a remarkable thing happened. I had gone to Southern

California, flying down in one of those monster jets. But when my visit ended, the airline was on strike and I had to return in a tiny plane. It coasted through the air quite slowly and quietly, and we could really see the Santa Lucia mountains not far below us. Suddenly the most marvelous sight struck my vision: A lovely little bridge, almost fairy-like or butterfly-like in its delicacy, spanned a canyon with the glorious, shining Pacific behind it. My heart was moved. It

Woodcut of the bridge done by the author in the late 1930s.

was MY BRIDGE. It was Bixby Creek Bridge — once called Rainbow Bridge. Suddenly I was home. Surely this was the most beautiful bridge in the world — why had it taken me so long to realize it?

It's been 50 years now since the ribbon was cut at Rainbow Bridge, a beautiful structure I cannot really claim as mine. It belongs to the world.

A Wild Coast and Lonely

The title of this book, *A Wild Coast & Lonely*, is taken from the *Ballad of the South Coast* by Lillian Bos Ross, known to her friends as Shanagolden. Lillian Bos Ross is best known as the author of *The Stranger* and *Blaze Allen.* Permission to reprint it here was given by her widower, Harrydick Ross.

The Ballad of the South Coast
by Shanagolden
(printed by permission of Harrydick Ross)

> *My name is Lonjano de Castro,*
> *My father was a Spanish grandee;*
> *But I won my wife in a card game—*
> *To hell with those lords o'er the sea!*
>
> *In my youth I had a Monterey homestead,*
> *Creeks, valleys, and mountains all mine;*
> *I built me a snug little shanty*
> *And I roofed it and floored it with pine.*
>
> *I had a bronco, a buckskin —*
> *Like a bird he flew over the trail;*
> *I rode him out forty miles every Friday*
> *Just to get me some grub and some mail.*
>
> *(Chorus)*
>
> *But the South Coast's a wild coast and lonely;*
> *You might win at a game at Jolon,*
> *But the lion still rules the barranca,*
> *And a man there is always alone.*
>
> *I sat in a card game at Jolon;*
> *I played with a half-breed named Juan,*
> *And after I'd won all his money*
> *He said "Your homestead 'gainst my*
>   *daughter Dawn."*

The Ballad of the South Coast

Music by Sam Eskin

I turned up the ace - I had won her!
My heart, which was down in my feet,
Jumped up to my throat in a hurry —
Like a young summer's day she was sweet.

He opened the door to the kitchen;
He called the girl in with a curse.
"Take her, God damn her, you've won her,
She's yours now, for better or worse!"

Her arms had to tighten around me
As we rode up the hills from the south,
But no word did I get from her that day,
nor a kiss from her pretty red mouth.

(Chorus)

We got to my cabin at twilight,
The stars twinkled over the coast.
She soon loved the orchard, the valley,
But I knew that she loved me the most.

That was a glad happy winter;
I carved at a cradle of pine
By the fire in that snug little shanty,
and I sang with that gay wife of mine.

But then I got hurt in a landslide,
Crushed hip and twice broken bone;
She saddled up Buck just like lightning,
And rode out through the night to Jolon.

(Chorus)

A lion screamed in the barranca;
Buck bolted and fell on a slide.
My young wife lay dead in the moonlight;
My heart died that night with my bride.

They buried her out in the orchard.
They carried me out to Jolon.
I've lost my chiquita, my niño;
I'm an old, broken man, all alone.

The cabin still stands on the hillside,
Its doors open wide to the wind,
But the cradle and my heart are empty -
I never can go there again.

(Chorus)

Sea Otter, Rarity Nowadays Along Coast, Returns

Treasure of Olden Times Rides Waves South of Carmel

By "UNCLE JOE" DEARING

A California treasure long believed lost has been found riding the blue, white-capped waves along the rugged shore line south of Carmel.

"Sea otter!" The magic word that first brought Spanish and Russian traders to the California coast is on the excited lips of everyone in that district.

"From nowhere" one hundred and sixty of these extremely valuable and remarkable mammals have appeared in the kelp beds along the Monterey County coast from Bixby Creek to Torre Canyon, a distance of eighteen miles.

$500,000 Worth

That many have actually been counted by Division of Fish and Game Warden Charles Mayfield, who has "lived" with the otters since they were first discovered.

There they feed and play in their inimitable and amusing way to bring life to an important page of early California history. Hundreds of spectators watch them daily from the high cliffs towering over their new found home.

The dark brown, frosted appearing pelts of this group would bring well over half a million dollars if sold at the last quoted price of $3,500 each. So fine is their fur that skins brought from $100 to $500 when the animal was plentiful along the Pacific Coast from Trinidad Bay south to lower California more than a hundred years ago.

Big Industry

History tells us that during the last quarter of the eighteenth century sea otters were the most important factor in the management of California by the Spanish nation. Their hunting constituted the only really important industry on the California coast for a third of a century.

Exploring expeditions sent out from San Blas, Mexico, in 1784, 1788 and 1790, stopped along the California coast to barter with Indians for otter skins. Their articles of trade were beads, pieces of iron, knives and cloth.

Abalone shells picked up by the thousands on the beaches near Monterey were traded for pelts farther north. Natives of the northwest coast would give the finest otter skin for one or two of the iridescent shells.

Were Plentiful

The Spaniards collected the skins from the natives through the missions, had them baled and sent to Mexico. There they were tanned and shipped to China to be exchanged for quicksilver, which was greatly needed to operate the Mexican mines.

In 1812 the Russians who settled at Fort Ross began exploring the coast, islands and arms of San Francisco Bay. They gathered great numbers of sea otter skins.

Sea otters at that time were particularly plentiful about the Farallone Islands, among the Channel Islands and in San Francisco Bay. One early manuscript—that of Valdez—says "they were so abundant in 1812 that they were killed by boatmen with their oars in passing through the kelp."

Rare After 1906

The great value of the sea otter's fur caused its wholesale destruction. They were considered extremely rare in 1906. They were seen for the last time, previous to their recent appearance, on October 23, 1914, when P. R. Greer reported two basking in the sun on the kelp beds off Del Monte.

The rate of reproduction in the sea otter is low. Usually only one young is born at a time.

Young otters can't swim and when the parents dive for food they are left floating on their backs on the surface.

The animal is noted for the great solicitude shown by the female for her young. When traveling, she swims on her back, carrying her young clasped between her forepaws.

Sea otters spend their entire lives in the sea, usually near some rocky shore line where their food—mussels, clams, abalones, sea urchins and other mollusks—are plentiful. They swim, play and dive for food during the daytime, under their backs then sleep under their chins on well, following kelp beds at night.

Sea otters, whose pelts are as valuable as their area covered with twenty-dollar bills, have returned to the California coast, below Carmel, after scientists had written "extinct" after their name. The above picture shows a fortune in shimmering brown, frosted-appearing fur. Excessively shy and their senses very acute, sea otter are extremely difficult to approach. Note how some are standing up in the water to investigate a slight sound made by Photographer Joe Dearing. Others lazily swim on their backs in regular fat man fashion. They spend their entire lives in the sea, feeding by day, sleeping in a real "cradle of the deep"—soft, buoyant kelp beds—at night. Hours of stalking and lots of luck resulted in this page of exclusive pictures, which includes the first closeups of sea otters ever taken in their natural habitat.

Here is the largest congregation of sea otters seen in more than a hundred years. The herd makes its home where Bixby Creek flows into the Pacific, sixteen miles south of Monterey. Abalones and other mollusks are plentiful here and it is hoped the valuable mammals will remain.

Division of Fish and Game Warden Charles E. Mayfield, custodian of the sea otter, helped transport The Call-Bulletin's "Big Bertha" down the 1,000 foot cliff, where stalking of the wary seafaring animals took place.

LAW PROTECTS SEA OTTERS

Sea otters have the full protection of the law. Anyone found injuring or killing them will face a tremendous fine or imprisonment. The herds at Carmel are guarded day and night by Division of Fish and Game officers.

Of all the wild life that was once California's, theirs is the only habitat that hasn't been at least partially destroyed by the inroads of civilization. It is hoped that by careful protection, the time may come when a limited number of furs may be harvested annually.

Otter (right) at favorite pastime—eating. Swimming on their backs, they hold their food in their fore paws. The crusted old boy in the right foreground is just finishing up an abalone he pulled off a rock at the bottom of sea.

Howard G. Sharpe, who discovered the extremely valuable and once believed extinct sea otter at Hurricane Point, which is overlooked by his telescope-equipped porch. Sharpe's find was verified by Dr. [...] old Heath, director emeritus of the Hopkins Marine Laboratory at Monterey, after several scientists refused to believe him.

Rarest Camera 'Scoop'

Closeups of 'Extinct' $500,000 Sea Otter Herd Off Monterey Shown by Telephoto Lens

The San Francisco Call Bulletin, May 14, 1938

XV. APPENDIX

The Sea Otter

by Howard G. Sharpe

This article on the re-discovery of the supposedly extinct southern sea otter on March 19, 1938, by my father had been amongst my papers all these years and I did not discover it until just before its fiftieth anniversary — which, oddly, coincided with the fifth birthday of my youngest granddaughter, Juliette.

My father had been a writer most of his life, but his father, a colonel, had insisted on an army career and, to take it up, he had to abandon a reporter's job on the Denver Post. He wrote adventure stories (in the same era as Edgar Rice Burroughs, Zane Grey and Jack London) and in, I believe, 1916 won the Harvard prize for the best short story of the year. I still have it. It is called, "The Sentry Box".

—Rosalind Sharpe Wall

The Discovery of the
"Extinct" Sea Otters

by Howard Granville Sharpe

"How did you discover the sea otter herd?" Many such questions are asked of me. At the time of the discovery, March 19, 1938, I owned a small ranch on the rugged coast 13 miles south of Carmel.

On my front porch, at cliff-edge, stood a powerful telescope commanding sea and shore. From 300 feet elevation it swept Discovery Cove and Sharpe's Point. Jutting into the ocean, this promontory forms a cove.

In a busy day I found no time for systematic scope-gazing, but might succumb if only to inspect some passing ship, or an outlying rock "Lady Kay". On this historic morning I had no definite object, but I wondered if Lady Kay would be weeping. If brine rivulets coursed her cheeks, a truculent tide was slapping her face.

I scanned kelp beds lying farther inshore. Slight movements there seemed inconsistent with normal rise and fall. I had no premonition that I was verging on a discovery destined to draw an army of spectators from the farthest reaches of the Earth. Certainly I couldn't know that I would find a cool million dollars in furs, or be the first to gaze at a sight unseen by mortals in a century.

***

To "Coasters" living in rugged Bixby Creek Canyon, objects riding the swell in a high tide aren't kelp. Today such float was visible, objects too uniform in size for the usual flotsam. Movement obviously was independent of the tide. Were they alive? Heads larger than kelp-bulbs resembled seal, sleek bodies seemed fur-bearing. But here similarities ended. What were those odd shaped flippers that seemed to grow from their backs? One object wriggled and turned over, then I realized that all the rest were inverted, lazy on their backs in patches of yellow-brown kelp. Distance from a sandy beach at Bixby Creek mouth was scarcely 120 yards.

Could they be walrus? Perhaps some odd species, fooled by a severe winter, mistook California for Alaska? No tusks? Then perhaps a "half fish, half horse, half alligator" had Davy Crocketted up from unexplored seas. These creatures were undeniably fur-bearers...

A strange excitement took hold of me. Puzzle: what salt water creature lies luxuriously on its back, hind legs sticking straight up, forelegs folded on its chest or muzzle? Some kind of otter?

I remembered a personal encounter with a land-otter in the Far East long ago. It was a far cry from that steaming episode in a tropical lake on Mindanao in the Philippines to my balcony at Rainbow Headlands. But I was determined to know, little dreaming how much there was to know and that it would make me the target for rifle bullets within a few days. Yes, indeed. The world might never have heard of my discovery but for my remembrance of that land otter episode.

The idea of this large herd of fur-bearers being genuine sea otters didn't, couldn't occur to me, because the myriads once thriving in kelp along the coast were all dead. Such at least was the scientific verdict. In other words "Southern Sea Otter" described as "Latax", or "Nehydra Lutris Nereis Merriam," were definitely wiped off scientific records, to fill a niche in natural history with a freakish group as dead as dodos. Could they be prehistoric, up from ocean depths?

If I tired of scope-gazing, the little rascals proved a magnet drawing me back. I called to a young employee:

"Do you see what I see?"

Did he? A strange question in the midst of workday affairs. But his good nature took over, he saw even more, not only verifying my "spike tails and four genuine legs instead of flippers," but he saw that the feet were partly webbed, five nails to each foot, faces like "muskrats." Also, an outlying group mistaken by me for kelp, was animal life instead. This brought my estimate up to more than 300 of the amazing creatures. Later, when my family members arrived I showed them the discovery.

The next person to see the extraordinary sight was a Mr. Frank Miller who chanced to drive out from Monterey. The press had it: A countryman discovered the sea otters, but Captain Lippincott, of the Fish & Game Commission, who happened to be passing told him that they were..."

It was two days later that on a trip to town we reported the discovery to Hopkins Marine Station. Everywhere we met a skepticism quite understandable even when tinged with amusement:

"Seals...Sea Lions...Nothing else."

Ditto four officials of the Fish and Game Commission. Our "find" left them cold. Also, three newspaper editors must have "seen no merit in our contention," for not a word appeared on a subject which, within three days, was to become world news astounding, and within limits of natural science "the scoop of the century."

Two days later we paid a second call on Fish & Game, with the same result.

"Can't possibly be anything but seals or sea lions," was the considered verdict. Veteran officer Captain Lippincott asked:

"How do you know they aren't seals or sea lions?"

This attitude swatted my self esteem rather rudely. I replied:

"They don't look like seals...nor sea lions."

By now I should have realized that my layman's opinions weren't worth much. I ran across Mr. (Frank) Miller who told me that his reports met with like skepticism.

Lippincott pondered over my story. Next morning with three juniors he appeared at Rainbow Headlands at my ranch. They peered through the scope; there came an odd silence. One officer wiped the lens, peered again. Lippincott backed away, hand across eyes. Looking at the object glass he adjusted the eyepiece to shorter focus. Gradually his body grew taut; voice came in a sharp whisper

"Sea otters...sea-OTTERS!"

Finally I asked: "Are you sure?"

"How could I mistake? There can be no doubt!"

"But they're all dead...extinct...years ago?"

Lippincott smiled grimly. In years of service he had seen freak happenings. Truly a new chapter in natural history was about to be written: the "impossible" had happened. A supposedly extinct animal came to life utterly without warning; a large herd with a cool million dollars in pelts, first time in history. Nature's immutable law was: "Once extinct; always extinct..." Of species dying out in our particular epoch: great auk and dodo by 1800, Mississippi Valley pigeon; Martha's Vineyard sage-hen; there was no question of the accuracy of the diagnosis. But these were all birds, whereas bison, West Coast hyena, and the sperm whale never quite vanished. The only four-legged creature universally canceled from the books in our time was the sea otter. My requests for herd guards to prevent sniping from the Coast Highway, and a patrol boat at the two-mile limit for poachers were acceded to at once. The Albatross was the vigilant launch chosen.

Hopkins Marine staff appeared, looked, apologized. Dr. Heath said:

"Had you reported dinosaurs or ichtysaurs running down your canyon swimming about, we couldn't have been more utterly dumfounded."

Whence came Southern sea otters? Not from the Aleuts. The few sea otters still found there belonged to the other existing species. The only known herd of Southern sea otters lay right at my doorstep.

***

My suggestion that they hid in Rainbow Headlands caverns was only less plausible than "so vast a herd hid in kelp, undiscovered for ages!"   One tunnel ramified through a hundred feet and pierces Rainbow Headlands from North to Discovery Cove, Bixby Creek mouth.

The problem remained a staggering mystery. Not since R. Chapman Andrews found dinosaur eggs in Mongolia was there such a contribution to the scientific world, or a reversal of judgment of such proportions. From all over the world writers pilgrimaged to this near-Mecca, Rainbow Headlands. Newsreel crews soon followed. This find wasn't in far off Mongolia, but right here in California.

The questions often recurred: "How did you discover the sea otters?" I was laughingly accused of rearing them in a trout-hatchery in my canyon, or importing them from Mars and suddenly springing them on a sensation-loving world.

Weeks after the discovery, a killer whale appeared within 80 feet of Bixby Creek mouth. The herd dived; scattered. Some 90 animals took up residence in Kelp Cove directly north of Rainbow Headlands, but too near shore for safety, the state highway lying some 200 feet above. Despite guard-vigilance a score of empty cartridge shells were found at the cliff edge. Four days later my son, William, a teen-ager, nearly caught some poachers. When I joined him we found a dead sea otter, bullet through its spine, washed up on the beach.

We turned it over to the Fish & Game Commission, but not before being sniped at from the bushes and the car in which the poachers fled.

On July 4 so many cannon crackers were hurled from the cliff that the patient little creatures wrinkled up their faces in startled abhorrence of Genus Homo and all his works and faded from sight, some to appear in the kelp a mile north, others to Discovery Cove. Meantime another section teemed with excitement: dozens appeared in the wave-slapped kelp off Torre Canyon, 15 miles south. Gradually their numbers diminished. Few of the herd remained at Torre Canyon. The 1958 census reported 600 sea otters scattered over wide areas.

How can a traveler know the difference between sea otters and land otters? Land otters greatly outnumber sea otters. They live on land, hunt in rivers and lakes. Sea otters, about twice the size, live exclusively on and in salt water. Seals have only flippers, sea otters four true legs and are more closely related to dogs or bears than are seals or sea lions.

Sea otters gestation period is nine months, not the three of land otter, sea, sea lion. Multiple birth is rare.

Unlike walrus and other ocean-going animals, sea otters have no set breeding seasons. Offspring arrive at about two-year intervals, the cute, furry ball born in kelp bobbing on the ocean swells. Held on its mother's belly for weeks, it is then taught to swim.

I've been asked: "Are sea otters too lazy to react like humans?" Say rather that they have a Stevensonian philosophy (Robert Louis), no quarrelling, no duelling, no bullying, no sex jealousies.

***

Rarely molested in kelp by sharks or killer whales, sea otters live like a Herman Melville Utopia, males all free-lance bachelors; females neither gold diggers nor party girls. They may have a technique of their own, these coy and demure, wholly self-satisfied sea otter queens of destiny.

Mating is neither seasonal nor weekend, just a whim of a moment it seems, always with a different mate. In one group of 80 — there are seldom more in one group — two or three of the largest have grizzled heads. One patriarch is all white, an albino. Another proudly wears a "white lion rampant" on chest and flanks. These seldom budged from Discovery Cove to chase after false kelp beds. Their titles fit them: Emperor; empress; a third whitish one of Discovery Cove falls heir to Archduke, Kronprinz.

Sea otter food is largely abalone, crab, sea urchin, shellfish from the ocean bed directly below their "parking places".`

After eating comes the siesta, if the day is sunny and warm, and ocean swells not too lusty. The really important activity is the bano (bath); whether a delousing process, or are they pestered by marine fleas? They scrub thoroughly all over. One powerful leg and foot is thrust vigorously up and down the spine like a Fuller brush.

***

Sea-otter ability to use tools: A hungry sea otter brings an abalone and a flat stone from the bottom, places the stone on its chest and hammers the shell fish against it with incredible speed. This makes the "click" sometimes heard. A small arc being broken from the shell, the meat is readily gouged out and eaten.

The rejected shell is customarily pounced on by a seagull which, at first click, wings its direct way to the scene of the banquet. The optimistic gull perches on neighboring kelp, bobs up and down to wait expectantly. Discovery Cove law: only one gull to an otter.

Among military campaigns noted for wholesale slaughter, one waged by the Russians till 1831 changed North American maps, determined the course of westward empire. To include it in "World's Decisive Battles" is impossible, for the victims weren't human but dumb animals.

Wealthy Russians and Spaniards as well as Chinese would wear no other furs. Higher quotations told the story of diminishing supply. Buccaneers cast greedy eyes at "Russia's private racket" and began to colonize in imitation of Russia's Fort Ross. California's matchless furs became the prize in the desperate scrabble.

***

A sea otter herd, said to be the last, took refuge in kelp coves of Monterey Peninsula and was annihilated presumably by 1831, according to Captain J. B. R. Cooper. Belated specimens were reported in 1908, 1916, some miles down the coast from Carmel, near Bixby Creek mouth. But were they seals?

A London scientific article (1938) states: ..."regrettable that no authentic picture of a sea-otter herd ever will be taken...Latax Lutris Nereis has been dead as a herd since 1831...

On the heels of this sage prophecy came my sensational find of March 19, 1938. When such pelts were legal, the latest quotes were $3,500.

In my books the most astounding mystery is: Where did the sea otter live for 107 years? In Rainbow Headlands caves? No. These caves are filled with water half the time. Sea otters need air. Did they hibernate? This and much else remain staggering mysteries. Will they ever be solved?

Nepenthe

July 8, 1989

Book Signing

A WILD COAST AND LONELY—Big Sur Pioneers

by Rosalind Sharpe Wall

It seems fitting that this book signing be held at Nepenthe, for it was at this site, in the summer of 1946, that I started doing research on my book and commenced the actual writing of it. I lived nearby in the Deetjen barn about a mile south of here. This is now Big Sur Inn, but in 1946 it was just a simple three story red barn complete with dust and cobwebs.

The Log House, the meeting place of the Coastlands Trails Club, stood here and was vacant that summer. It had been built by Sam Trotter in the early 1920's for the newly arrived Coastlands Association, most of whom were Christian Scientists.

Trotter, a master woodsman, had arrived at the height of the tanbark and lumber era of the 1890's and married Adelaide Pfeiffer, the statuesque and beautiful daughter of the earliest pioneers to come down the coast trail to Big Sur. Michael and Barbara Pfeiffer had come to Sycamore Canyon in 1869 and never left.

And so somehow, from the very beginning, the Log House — which still exists and is just behind and above this terrace — formed a symbolic bridge between the past and future. Newcomers were thus linked to the pioneers through Sam Trotter's superb workmanship.

In 1944, the avant-garde writer Henry Miller turned up penniless and in need of haven, and was invited to stay at the Log House by its tenant, Lynda Sargent, also a writer. Henry was working on the The Air Conditioned Nightmare. When suddenly a bombshell burst upon them. The Coastlands Association had sold the Log House to Orson Welles as a gift for Rita Hayworth. The whole coast was furious. Indeed, they were very snobbish about movie stars, which is to say a reverse snobbism, although they had grudgingly accepted Ronald Colman who had bought property below Big Sur in 1926.

Henry Miller wrote a furious invective and curse against the intruders from the movie world. And perhaps it worked, for Orson Welles and Rita Hayworth never moved into the place and indeed never even saw it.

Then, in 1947, it was bought by Bill and Lolly Fassett. The Fassetts with their five children, Griff, Kaffe, Dorcas, Holly and Kim, moved into the Log House while commencing to build Nepenthe, which had been Lolly's dream — or "brain-storm" as she would have termed it. They all went to work making adobe bricks for the construction of the restaurant to be. As soon as it opened, Nepenthe immediately became a gathering place for writers and artists, and many were the tourists who flocked there to see the members of the famed art colony in person, drinking beer and eating ambrosia burgers. Lolly Fassett, who played hostess, always wore long Chinese tunics and silken slacks and dangling Chinese earrings, usually of jade. She sold beer at a dollar a pitcher to denizens of the art colony since they added so much atmosphere and these people, including Henry Miller, were indeed too poor to pay more.

The name Nepenthe, which was Lolly's inspiration, came from Homer and meant nectar of the gods but also forgetfulness, like the waters of Lethe — but these were not the waters of death, rather of ecstatic oblivion.

But back to the beginning. It does seem very fitting that the book signing party be here because the beauty that is focussed here and indeed visibly and overwhelmingly surrounds us as we look at the mountains and down to the sea below — transcends time. Beauty is always timeless. Beauty is forever. Beauty is. Today, yesterday, tomorrow — there is no difference. People come and go as people always do and have done through the milleniums.

But here at Nepenthe, Lolly's "brain storm" holds beauty like a jewel in a cup for all to behold.

As Lolly remarked one moonlit night on the terrace, "You know, I have always had the feeling about this place that I didn't create anything but just brought out something that was already here — that pre-existed and was built into this land. This is the magic people feel at Nepenthe."

—Rosalind Sharpe Wall

Suggested Reading

Those who wish to delve further into the lore of the Sur as depicted in poetry, fiction, memories, and prose may find much of the following valuable. Not all of it is equally recommended, however e.g., John Kerouac's book, *Big Sur*, is a curiosity of the Beatnik era but does not depict the Sur, and Dan Totheroh's *Deep Valley* is of dubious literary merit. The work of Robinson Jeffers is, of course, especially endorsed for its reflection of the spirit and beauty of the landscape and the timeless nature of its classic themes.

Bennett, Melba Berry. *Robinson Jeffers and the Sea.* San Francisco, Folcroft Library Edition. 1973.

Bennett, Melba Berry. *The Stone Mason of Tor House The life and work of Robinson Jeffers.* Foreward by Lawrence Clark Powell. Ward Ritchie, Orinda, California. 1966.

Brautigan, Richard. *A Confederate General from Big Sur.* Grove Press, N.Y. 1964.

Brooks, Van Wyck. *Scenes and Portraits.* Dutton, 1954.

Chase, J. Smeaton. *California Coast Trails.* Houghton Mifflin Co., Boston. 1913.

De Angulo, Gui. *Jaime in Taos.* City Lights Books, San Francisco. 1985.

De Angulo, Jaime. *Indian Tales.* Hill & Wang, New York. 1953.

De Angulo, Jaime. *Coyote Man and Old Doctor Loon.* Turtle Island, Berkeley. 1973.

De Angulo. *Coyote's Bones.* Selected poetry and prose edited by Bob Callahan. Turtle Island Foundation, San Francisco. 1974.

De Angulo, Jaime. *Don Bartolomeo.* Turtle Island, San Francisco. 1974.

De Angulo, Jaime. *How the World was Made.* Turtle Island, Berkeley. 1976.

De Angulo, Jaime. *Shabegok.* Turtle Island, Berkeley. 1974.

Delkin, James Ladd. *Monterey Peninsula.* Compiled by workers of the writer's project of the Works Progress Administration in Northern California. James Ladd Delkin, Stanford University Press. 1946.

Georgette, Susan E. *In the Rough Land to the South, an Oral History of the Lives and Events of Big Creek, Big Sur, California.* Environmental Field Publications #5, University of California (Santa Cruz). 1981.

Goodman, Judith, editor, and Addleman, Pat, designer. *Big Sur Women.* Judith Goodman Big Sur Women Press, Big Sur, California. 1985.

Hale, Sharron Lee. *A Tribute to Yesterday: The History of Carmel Valley, Big Sur, Point Lobos, Carmelite Monastery, and Los Burros.* Valley Pub., 1980.

Jeffers, Robinson. *The Selected Poetry of Robinson Jeffers.* Randon House, New York. 1951.

Jeffers, Robinson. *Californians.* Macmillan. 1916.

Jeffers, Robinson. *The Jeffers Country: The seed plots of Robinson Jeffers' poetry.* Poetry by Robinson Jeffers. Photos by Horace Lyon. Scrimshaw Press, San Francisco. 1971.

Jeffers, Robinson. *Not Man Apart, photographs of the Big Sur Coast.* Lines from Robinson Jeffers. Photos by Ansel Adams and others. Ed. by David Brower. Sierra Club. 1965.

Jeffers, Robinson. *Thurso's Landing and other poems.* Liveright. 1932.[1]

Jeffers, Una (Call) Kuster. (Mrs. Robinson Jeffers.) Greenan, Edith. *Of Una Jeffers.* (decorations by Fletcher Martin). Ritchie. 1939.

Kerouac, John. *Big Sur.* Farrar, Straus, Cudahy. 1962.

Kroeber, A.L. *Handbook of the Indians of California.* U.S. Government Printing Office, Washington, D.C. 1925.

Lussier, Tomi Kay. *Big Sur: A Complete History and Guide.* Big Sur Publications. 1979.

Luhan, Mabel Dodge. *Una and Robin.* Edited, with a foreward by Mark Schorer. The Friends of the Bancroft Library, University of California. 1976.

McWilliams, Carey. *Southern California Country.* Chapter 2; "The Indian in the Closet." Duell, Sloan and Pearce, New York. 1946.

Miller, Henry. *A Devil in Paradise. The Story of Conrad Moricand.* New American Library, New York. 1956.

Miller, Henry. *Big Sur and the Oranges of Heironmymous Bosch.* New Directions Publishing Corp., New York. 1957.

Mitchell, Ruth Comfort. *Corduroy Road.* Appleton, Century Crofts, New York. 1923.

Ogden, Adelle. *The California Sea Otter Trade* 1784-1848. University of California Press. 1941.

Powell, Lawrence Clark. *Robinson Jeffers: The man and his work.* A foreward by Robinson Jeffers; decorations by Rockwell Kent. The Primavera Press, Los Angeles. 1934.

Ross, Lillian Bos. *Blaze Allen.* William Morrow. 1944.

Ross, Lillian Bos. *The Stranger.* Capra Press, Santa Barbara. 1985.[2]

Sanchez, Nelko Van der Grift. *Spanish and Indian Place Names of California.* Self-published. San Francisco, 1914.

Totheroh, Dan. *Deep Valley.* L.B. Fischer. 1942. [2]

Walker, Franklin. *The Sea Coast of Bohemia.* Peregrine-Smith, Inc. 1973.

Woolfenden, John, *Big Sur: A Battle for the Wilderness.* The Boxwood Press, Pacific Grove, California. 1985.

Woolfenden, John and Elkinton Amelie. *Cooper: Juan Bautista Rogers Cooper.* The Boxwood Press, Pacific Grove, California. 1983.

Young, Ella. *Flowering Dusk.* Longmans, Green and Co., New York, Toronto. 1945.

---

[1] *Thurso's Landing* is not singled out as being superior to the other narrative poems, but because it is referred to in the text and is an integral part of it.

[2] These two novels were made into films.

As a young woman, "Down Coaster" Rosalind Sharpe Wall left The Sur to major in anthropology at Reed College. Upon her return, she was locally known as a newspaperwoman and was associated for many years with the Carmel *Pine Cone* and *Game and Gossip* magazine. Wall was awarded an M.A. in English from Sonoma State University in 1984. She also authored *About Jeanie D'Orge and Carl Cherry*, which she donated to the Cherry Foundation. With John Cooke, she co-authored two books on Tarot. In addition to being a writer, Rosalind Sharpe Wall was an artist. She died in 1991.